TEN ADVE

WALKS IN

SURREY

Raymond Hugh

Illustrations by
Jackie Hei

ISBN 1 874476 00 4

2nd edition
First Published 1992
This edition Morning Mist Publishing 1993
P.O. Box 108, Reigate, Surrey RH2 9YP.

Designed and Printed by
Advanced Data Graphics, Sevenoaks

INDEX

INTRODUCTION

THE ADVENTURE

The adventure must be yours, it is the thrill of exploration, the pleasure of experiencing something new and the surprise of the unexpected. You could do the same walk several times and each time it will different. One time a deer may bound across your path, another time a squirrel leap high above your head, on one day you can see miles across the Surrey Weald and on another the mist hides the trees only a few feet away. The weather cannot only change the appearance of a walk, it can also change the feel. The adventure is discovering the secrets of the route on the day.

THE REWARD

To commemorate your achieving one of the walks, a sew-on badge is available direct from the publisher. To claim a badge send an account of your walk in no more than one hundred words, together with a cheque or postal order, payable to Morning Mist Publishing, for £3.25. This includes postage and packing. Address: Morning Mist Publishing, P.O. Box 108, Reigate, Surrey, RH2 9YP. Please allow 28 days..

WHEN TO GO

Many walkers make the mistake of only walking in fine weather, leaving the hills at the slightest sign of rain. In wet and windy weather the countryside is untamed and with the majority of the population safe in their houses, one can really get a feeling of remoteness and a better idea of what Surrey was like several hundred years ago. My suggestion is that you try and do the walks in all seasons and all weathers. At the end if you don't hate me, you will really begin to feel an affinity with the Surrey countryside and the satisfaction of knowing Surrey well. As for the time of day, I recommend that you try and time your walk to include either dawn or dusk. These to me are the best parts of the day, unfortunately often missed by the majority.

PREPARATION

Planning the walk is as important and as enjoyable as doing the walk itself. Firstly consider whether you want to make a weekend of it. If you do, then I suggest that you book local accommodation. This not only cuts down on travelling on the day, but creates a seemingly longer weekend and allows you to remain familiar with the area at night.

There is nothing better in my mind than to finish a long walk and retire to local accommodation for a hot bath before a well earned visit to the local village pub, without having to worry about driving home. A selection of recommended accommodation is listed at the end of each walk.

Once you have decided on your walk, familiarise yourself with it. Read the walk through, following it on the map, to ensure you understand where it is you are going. The route descriptions contain points of interest and you may want to take time to stop and visit these. If you do, it might be worth borrowing a book from the Library to read up before your visit. When you have made up your mind on the points of interest to visit, try and estimate the length of your walk. The timings given on each walk are meant as a rough guide only and are based on a person being reasonably fit. If you are unsure, then I suggest you allow for approximately two miles per hour. Timing is important as you could find yourself stumbling back to the start in the dark.

Finally, make sure you are fit, the walks in this book are longer than the average walking book and can be hard work if you are unprepared. To help identify the gradients, a cross section is included at the start of each walk.

WHAT TO TAKE

A good map is essential. I recommend you use the Ordnance Survey Landranger maps and the start of each walk details the map(s) required. You can also use the Ordnance Survey Pathfinder maps which have far more detail such as field boundaries, but they can be harder to find and can ultimately be more expensive.

Once armed with your map, make sure you have sensible clothing, this means clothes which are loose and comfortable. Tight jeans and high heels are not recommended! No matter how good the weather is at the start of the day, always pack some waterproofs. Being caught out in the rain without the necessary protection is not an experience I would recommend. In summer if you are walking in shorts, wateproof trousers are also particularly useful as a temporary protection against nettles. There is a wide range of waterproof clothing now available, the two recommendations I would make are:-

(1) Make sure you are completely covered, that is buy trousers and a jacket.

(2) Buy clothing made from one of the breathable materials - your local stockist will advise you on these.

If the weather is cold, then gloves and a hat are always advisable. No matter what time of year, I always pack a jumper and have never regretted it. Keeping warm helps avoid tiredness. Most importantly, make sure you have a good pair of shoes. If you can afford it, then buy a pair of walking boots. If not, then make sure your shoes are strong, comfortable and have soles with a good grip Equally important are good socks. If you have boots then two pairs are advisable. Do not think that the socks you wear in the office will do!

Sensibly clothed, you can now think about any other equipment you may need. A camera and a pair of binoculars are always useful and can enhance your day out. I always carry a pocket book on birds, you could do the same or add to this with a book on local flora or history. You will find the walk all the more enjoyable for a little bit of knowledge. Do not though get over enthusiastic and take a library or you may find yourself requiring a book on first aid!

A basic first aid kit though is always advisable. The Surrey countryside may appear tame and so it is compared to the Himalayas but must still be treated with respect. The book and the map should be enough to find the route without difficulty, however a compass is always useful for finding your way when paths are undefined.

Refreshments are always an important consideration. There are places where you can get a bite to eat on every walk but even if you wish to use their facilities it is important to carry some basic snacks, especially in cold weather. You should always carry water and a thermos flask with hot soup or drink can also be very welcome. To carry all this one should have a comfortable day sack or small rucksack. These are now available from a wide assortment of shops, but before you purchase one, make sure it's strong and more importantly ensure it's comfortable.

Finally, take your five senses with you - these are essential if you are to fully appreciate the walk and most importantly, **ENSURE YOU TAKE THIS BOOK!**

GETTING THERE

Most people will be mobile, i.e. a car or bicycle. Where practical I have listed railway stations, however buses are far more difficult as their routes and timetables tend to change with the wind. For those people relying on a bus to reach the start, I have listed the main bus companies serving the area below:-

London & Country (Tel: 081668 7268)
Minicruisers (Tel: 0342 844422)
Taxibus (Tel: 0306 884937)
Tillingbourne (Tel: 0483 276880)
W&H Motors Ltd (Tel: 0293 510220)

ROUTE FINDING

The route descriptions are instructional rather than poetic and should be followed without difficulty. To assist you a series of symbols in the left hand margin enable you to identify specific points on the walk at a glance. A good map is essential and should be used in conjunction with the route description. Please remember that like everything else, the countryside changes with time, a fenced path can become unfenced and vice versa.

Before setting out, make sure you have identified the route on the map. To pinpoint a starting point or place of interest I have used grid references. These are six figured numbers which identify a particular point on the map. Every Ordnance Survey map is covered by a national grid. The grid's lines are identified by numbers printed on the map's surround. To find a grid reference, take the first three numbers which refer to the vertical lines on your map and locate them on the top or bottom (north or south) of the map. The third number is an imaginary line in the square following the first two numbers. To find this line, divide the square into ten equal parts. Then take the last three numbers, which refer to the horizontal lines and locate them on the left or right (east or west) of your map and follow the line of this reference until it meets the line of the first reference. Their meeting point is the grid reference point itself. Do not rely on the maps in this book, these are not to scale and are meant as a rough guide only.

It is important that you recognise the various types of footpath signs. Most are fairly obvious, i.e. wooden post with a sign marked "footpath" or "public bridleway", pointing in the direction of the right of way. Some will have the name of a specific route, for example, "The North Downs Way."

Over recent years many County Councils have standardised their signs to follow national guidelines. Footpaths are now shown with a yellow arrow and bridleways with a blue one. Like the old wooden signs the arrows will point in the direction of the right of way. Some arrows will have the initials of a recognised walk imprinted, the most common one you will see is "GW", which marks the Greensand Way. On top of all this, you will often find custom built signs. These can mark an official route but more often than not, are the work of local farmers guiding the walker across their land. An example of the former, is "The North Downs Way", which is highlighted by a white acorn on a black background.

An important rule on route finding is to take your time, follow the map and read the route description thoroughly. If you do this, then you will return to base without mishap.

LONG DISTANCE WALKS

Many of the routes meet long distance linear walks which run through Surrey. In case you want to try any, I have listed their names with distances below, along with the publisher that produces a description of the walk.

Downs Link - 30 miles (West Sussex County Council)
Greensand Way -106 miles (Ramblers Association)
London Country Way - 205 miles (Constable)
North Downs Way -141 miles (HMSO)
Sussex Border Path -150 miles (Ben Perkins)
Vanguard Way - 63 miles (Ramblers Association)

AUTHOR'S NOTE

Every effort has been made to ensure that the route descriptions are accurate. Time changes things however and can alter the description of the route. If you have any difficulty in finding any part of a route, please write with details giving a grid reference to enable me to re-examine the route. A free copy of the next publication will be forwarded for any suggestions used in the next edition. Enjoy your walks.

THE LEITH HILL LIMP

Distance: 9½ miles (15.25 km)

Time: Allow approximately 4½ hours

Map: Ordnance Survey Landranger Map 187

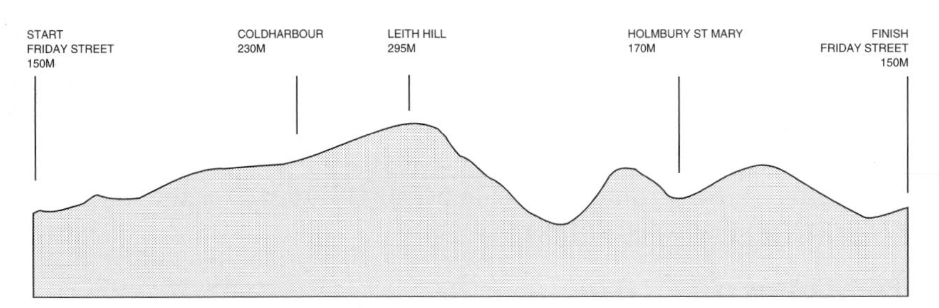

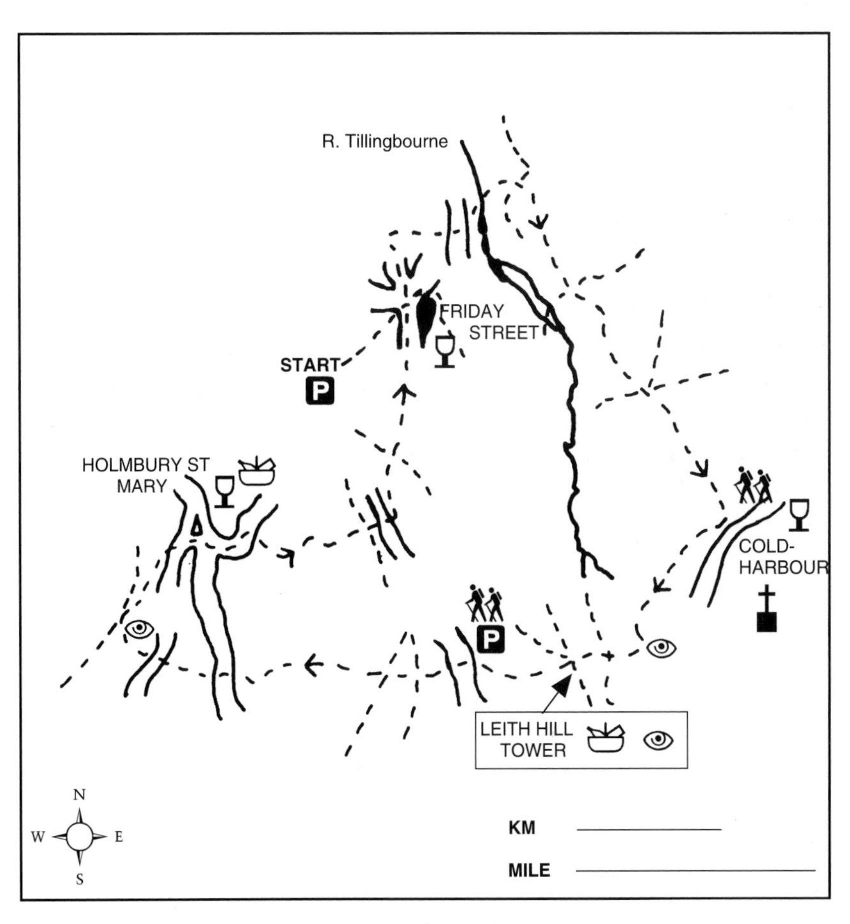

Walk Summary

A walk through the extensive woodlands of Holmbury and Leith Hill taking in the summit of Leith Hill itself. The only real respite from woodland are the two villages, Coldharbour and Holmbury St. Mary, once infamous smuggler haunts. The walker is rewarded with fine views and if alert, will enjoy the abundance of wildlife which the woods support. The going can be very muddy so good footwear is essential.

Start - OS. 126457 Map 187

The public car park at Friday Street. Follow the signs to Friday Street from the A25 or B2126. The car park is well signposted. Other alternative starting points are Coldharbour OS. 150440 or the car park for Leith Hill tower OS. 131434.

THE LEITH HILL LIMP

P From the car park walk back towards the road and take the footpath right downhill running parallel with the road. Go down some steps and join the road still going downhill, to meet the hammer pond at Friday Street. Turn left at the pond across the road to join a signposted public footpath passing a cottage on your right. Follow the track, crossing over a small ford via a rickety wooden footbridge and continue until the path forks. Take the left hand fork passing "Yew Tree" cottage and following the stream on your left which shortly fills out into a pond.

The pond is the creation of a small dam which also acts as a bridge and is a good if early opportunity to stop and appreciate the beauty of your surroundings. Do not cross the bridge but turn right over a stile to go uphill along a fenced path which at the top, bends round to the right with good views to your left of the North Downs.

After a short distance, the path bends round to the left (you cannot continue straight on as this is Wotton estate land). You soon reach a fork at which you should turn right leaving the main path to continue ahead through beech woods with a field on your right. On meeting a stile, cross this and the road to join the footpath opposite, which descends becoming steeper as you go. At the time of writing, this area is still suffering some years after the hurricane of 1987.

After passing through an avenue of laurels still going downhill, cross a stile into an open field with the Tillingbourne river on your right. Continue along a raised track to cross the river and go up towards a gate ahead. Just prior to the gate, cross the stile on your right and turn left along a wide track to pass a pond on your left. Shortly after the pond, the track bends round to the left where there is a footpath sign indicating you are on the Greensand Way "GW". Turn right at this sign on to a narrow footpath, which ascends slowly, running adjacent to a field on your left. At the far end of the field, cross over the remains of a stile taking time to catch your breath and admire the view.

Continue on over a small bank and then turn right along a wide track, between banks (this area can be extremely wet and muddy in bad weather). The track which is Wolvens Lane, leads you to Coldharbour village, a distance of approximately 3 miles. You must ensure you stay on the track, ignoring all crossing and joining tracks - do not be tempted to turn off!

Along the way, you will pass through dense coniferous woodland which at times can be quite haunting, Tankards pond on your right adjacent to a junction and sometime after, a cottage on your left. The woodland then becomes largely deciduous and you will pass an old disused loading platform before arriving at Coldharbour, the highest village in Surrey.

Coldharbour Village and Anstiebury Hill Fort (OS. 150440 Map 187). *Coldharbour perched high on the side of Leith Hill, is the highest village in Surrey and also boasts the highest cricket pitch in the county. Its setting is quite spectacular with just about every residence having a superb view across the Surrey Weald. Until late last century Coldharbour was a dangerous place renowned for smuggling. The wooded hills of this area known locally as Little Switzerland, were ideal for hiding contraband and yourself if the need arose - and it did! Often the smuggled merchandise would be buried safe from detection, the soft turf of the area making this option easiest and the most common. Occasionally, a local would stumble across such a hide and if this happened, he would mark certain items with a white cross and return them to their lair. The smuggler would then leave the marked items as a token of thanks for the silence of the finder. Apparently, the local villagers were sensible enough not to be too greedy.*

Coldharbour and Leith Hill were also renowned for highway men and it is reported that at their height even the greengrocer's cart carried a man armed with a blunderbuss. The tree lined hill behind "The Plough" pub is Anstiebury hill fort, once an iron age fort and one of the largest in Surrey. The fort is 247m high and covers 11 acres. It was protected by a ring of 3 banks and ditches. The fort is still sometimes referred to as Danes Fort or the Danish Camp after a famous victory over the Danes led by King Ethelwulf in 852AD. The Danes who were massacred are supposed to have sheltered at the hill fort on the eve of the battle. A large collection of human bones recently found on Leith Hill are believed to be the remains.

The fort was used again during the Napoleonic wars to protect the women and children of Coldharbour from the long suffering and revengeful residents of Dorking, the smugglers victims.

The church in Coldharbour is a relatively recent addition to the village, built in 1848 by one Benjamin Ferrey. For refreshments there is "The Plough" pub, a free house serving a wide range of food.

The track ends at the village where you should turn right between a telephone box and post box up a loose tarmac track, taking the right hand fork uphill at an "Emergency Access" sign. Look out for a bench on your left made from a fallen tree from the storm of 1987, where you can enjoy superb views over the Surrey Weald. Continue along the track ignoring all joining tracks to reach Coldharbour cricket pitch on your right, pass the gate to the pitch and take the left fork shortly after to join another wide track. Continue on the track to meet the remains of an ancient wall on your right, which you should follow for a short distance until you meet a prominent track on your left.

Take this track left passing through a young pine plantation to reach the perimeter of the hill in front of a wooden bench. Here there are more excellent views across the Surrey Weald.

Turn right following the perimeter of the hill to reach a junction and a footpath sign marked with a picture of a tower. Turn right in the direction of the tower sign, passing a wooden gate, to continue downhill on the main track. Turn left at a large crossroads of tracks, still following the signs to the tower, to go steeply uphill. The tower, owned by the National Trust, soon comes into view.

i

Leith Hill Tower 295m/965 feet (OS. 139431 Map 187)*, is the highest hill in Surrey. The tower on the top of the hill brings the total height of the hill to over 1000 feet above sea level, making Leith Hill even if it is man-made, the only mountain in the south east of England. The tower was built in 1776 by Richard Hull who lived in "Leith Hill Place". Years later during restoration his body was found bricked up inside the tower, this having been his dying wish.*

From the top of the tower, it is claimed you can see parts of 13 counties (bring a telescope!), you can certainly spot the main landmarks of London. Despite its popularity, Leith Hill remains a wild place and there is no better time to visit than on a stormy day when with the lack of other visitors one can really imagine what Surrey was like several hundred years ago. At the base of the tower there is a small serving hatch where tickets are sold to visit the top as well as light refreshments.

Pass in front of the tower going straight ahead descending gently down a wide track, ignoring all tracks going off to the left and right. Continue on this track for approximately three quarters of a mile, following the blue "GW" arrows until you meet a lane.

Cross the lane to join a bridleway the other side, again marked by the blue arrow "GW" sign. Go straight on and after a short distance, leave the Greensand Way as it bends right and continue downhill to reach a clearing with a large property visible on your left. Cross the clearing to continue straight ahead, ignoring the paths to your left and right.

The bridleway continues steeply downhill (ignore a lesser track later on your right), for a quarter of a mile to meet a stream and for a short distance, becomes one and the same. The going can be very wet in winter and you should therefore follow the bridleway signs where indicated to avoid the worst of the mud.

The path narrows and follows the line of a field with woodland on your right to shortly arrive at some farm buildings. Follow the path through the farm and turn right along the farm drive to reach a road. Turn left along the road for approximately 50 metres and turn right on to a footpath, crossing over a stile into a field. Cross a second stile and continue on a grass track leading into a field and walk gently uphill along the right hand perimeter to cross another stile on to a narrow fenced path.

Continue uphill to cross a small lane and join a path opposite with a considerable climb still ahead. As you near the top of the hill it is worth looking back to appreciate the views or alternatively stopping to collapse!

The path meanders through oak and birch trees to reach a wide track on to which you should turn right and continue on to a large junction of tracks where you should turn immediately right on to a footpath marked "GW", the Greensand Way, (not second right). The path shortly passes Holmbury cricket pitch on your left. Go straight on taking in good views on your right of your earlier route. Ignore the turning off to the left and continue winding downhill to reach a road by some houses, to turn left.

Should you wish to visit the centre of Holmbury St. Mary follow Holmbury Hill road. Turn left when this meets the main road and you will arrive at the village green.

Holmbury St. Mary (OS. 110444 Map 187). *Before Victorian times, Holmbury St. Mary was virtually a wilderness well known for its smugglers and other inhabitants of dubious repute. The village nestling in the shadow of Holmbury Hill looks a lot older than it actually is. Nearly all the buildings visible today are Victorian, including the church which was built in 1873. The church was designed and built by G. E. Street, a resident of Holmbury in his later years, who was the designer of the London Law Courts. He is now buried in Westminster Abbey. Before the church was built the village was called Felday. Holmbury St. Mary was adopted upon completion of the new church.*

The village still has a small chapel with the name of Felday. For refreshments the village boasts "The Royal Oak" pub, (Friary Meux). It has an attractive setting on the green and serves up a wide choice of good food.

To continue our route, go down the hill ignoring Holmbury Hill road on your left, passing "Pitman Street House" on your right. The Post Office ahead sells basic provisions. Just before this however on your left you will see "The Kings Head" pub, a free house, offering more substantial refreshments and most importantly a wide range of real ales!

Pass the Post Office and cross the main road ahead, turn right and then immediately left still following the Greensand Way. Pass "Bulmer Farm" on your left and continue up the road, taking care along the bend, ignoring the first bridleway on the right thereby leaving the Greensand Way.

Shortly after "Pasturewood Cottage", take the somewhat hidden footpath on your right going into the woods. The path, which is narrow, twists uphill through the trees to then run between banks, crossing a narrow grass path. On reaching a large oblong clearing go straight across entering the trees ahead of you (do not turn off). The path travels through dense, sometimes muddy, woodland going straight across two crossing paths to eventually meet a field. Turn right at the field and follow the perimeter to cross an unusual stile and continue straight ahead. On reaching a wide track, turn left to meet a "T" junction almost immediately thereafter.

Turn right and then immediately left on to a path leading to a farm gate through which you should pass. Follow the right hand perimeter of the field to cross a stile on to a narrow path leading gently downhill to a clearing before a road. Cross the road, turn left and directly opposite a large track and sign "Dorlin", turn right to take a very narrow footpath going downhill into the wood. At the bottom of the hill you will reach a crossroads at which you should turn left on to a wide track running between banks, in front of you as a guide is a small stone with an anchor and III. Continue along the track until you meet houses and then a road with a small pool and beginnings of a stream on your right.

This picturesque hamlet is Abinger Bottom. Turn left along the road and after 40 metres join a public bridleway on your right. Look out for an attractive footbridge on your right. Do not cross this but continue straight on for half a mile, following a muddy stream on your right and passing a second footbridge, to join a tarmac lane. This leads to Friday Street and "The Stephan Langton" pub and restaurant (Worthington).

***Friday Street (OS. 127456)**, has changed little over the centuries, its remote location protecting its beauty from modern development. The pub's name is a clue that Friday Street has a tale worth telling. The tale is of Stephan Langton, Archbishop of Canterbury during the reign of King John. Stephan was born at Friday Street in 1150. At the age of 10 his mother died and he was adopted by monks.*

Perhaps missing his family, Stephan left the monastery at the age of 18, to live with his aunt and cousin, Alice. Disaster struck when out travelling in the woods with his cousin, they were attacked by a gang of men, headed by the then Prince John. Alice was taken and inconsolable, Stephan spent all his time searching for her. Eventually he was rewarded. Alice was found at "Tangley Manor" (south of Chilworth in Surrey). In his rescue attempt, which involved setting fire to the house, Alice fainted. Close to capture himself, Stephan believed Alice to be dead and fled leaving her behind. A wanted man, Stephan left England and later returned a monk. His hard work and dedication was rewarded by his appointment to Archbishop of Canterbury.

Whilst Archbishop, Stephan returned to his roots and went to St. Martha's Chapel on St. Martha's Hill to celebrate mass. There to his surprise was his long lost cousin Alice. Unfortunately, the luckless Alice overcome by emotion collapsed and died on the spot. The name of the pub is now the only visible association with Stephan, not even a chapel stands in his honour. The pub though, is a worthy memorial and if you start the walk early enough you can return to enjoy a hearty lunch. The choice and quality of the food, which is home cooked, is excellent.

Continue down the lane noting the blue and yellow paintwork on the village houses, which denotes their being part of the Wotten estate. Pass the hammer pond on your right, to the end of the road where you should turn left to join the footpath beside the road leading you back to the car park, your starting point.

Accommodation

The Hurtwood Inn (THF), Peaslake. Tel: 0306 730851

Two miles from the walk, the Hurtwood Inn is a friendly relaxed hotel at the centre of village life with resident guests and local inhabitants mixing easily in an unpretentious bar. The surrounding countryside is only paces from the front door allowing for a pleasant evening stroll after the excesses of the evening.

Bulmer Farm, Holmbury St. Mary. Tel: 0306 730210

On the walk, Bulmer Farm is a lovely 17th century farmhouse offering first class accommodation at very reasonable prices. Guests can enjoy an attractive beamed lounge with log fires in winter and a large well planned garden. Bulmer Farm is in a good location if you wish to attempt "The Holmbury Hurt" and "The Leith Hill Limp" in one weekend.

Youth Hostel, Holmbury St. Mary. Tel: 0306 730777

One and a half miles from the walk, a purpose built youth hostel set in large attractive grounds. The setting is superb, take one step out of the grounds and you are in the extensive Hurtwood. The youth hostel can be busy in summer with school parties - so be warned. Camping is permitted in the grounds.

THE HOLMBURY HURT

Distance: 9½ miles (15.25 km)

Time: Allow approximately 4½ hours

Map: Ordnance Survey Landranger Map 187

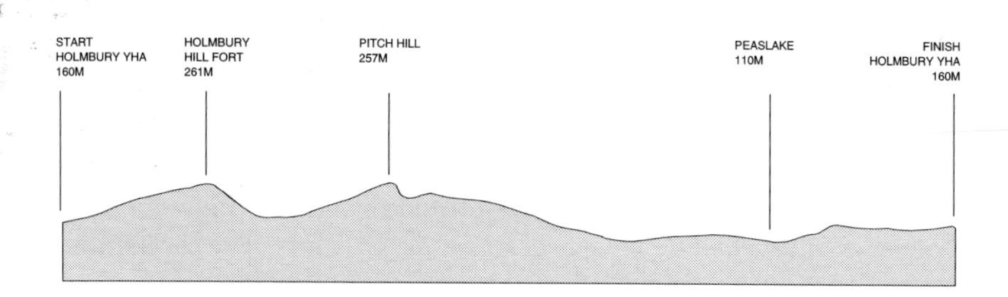

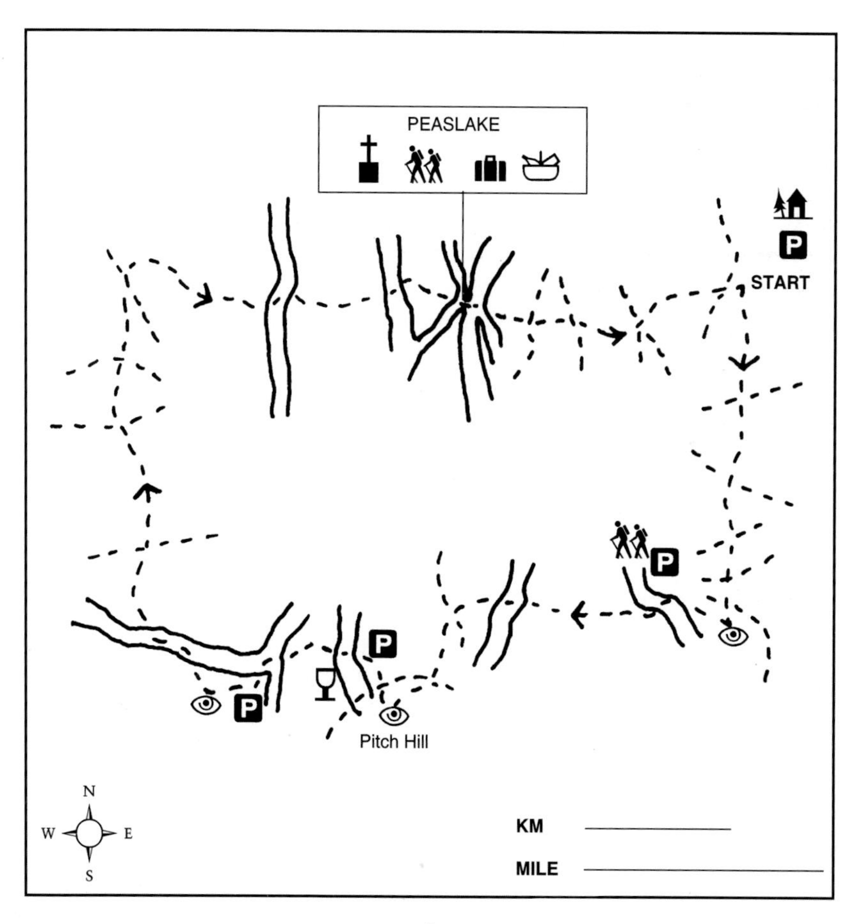

Walk Summary

The Holmbury Hurt explores the beautiful Hurtwood with its wealth of flora and fauna. Part of the walk follows the Greensand Way along the Greensand Ridge with superb views across the Surrey Weald to the South Downs. At the same time the route also takes some lesser known paths uncovering secrets missed by the many. The walk is fairly easy going, the biggest problem being the many woodland paths which insist on a careful study of the route if one is to avoid getting lost.

Start - OS. 105450 Map 187

The walk starts at the Hurtwood Control car park opposite the Holmbury St. Mary youth hostel. To get there take the B2126, the youth hostel is signposted on the western side of the road between the hamlet of Sutton and the village of Holmbury St. Mary. The car park is at the end of a long narrow lane. Other good starting points, are the Holmbury Hill car park at Coverwood (OS. 099432 Map 187) or at Peaslake (OS. 087447 Map 187).

THE HOLMBURY HURT

P

From the Hurtwood Control car park, take the path straight ahead going south, leaving the youth hostel directly behind you. Do not turn left or right.

i

Hurtwood. *As you start you will see several woodland signs headed Hurtwood Control. The beautiful Hurtwood which you are about to explore, was donated to the public by Reginald Bray of Shere in 1926 for, in his words, "air and exercise". The Hurtwood Control Committee, was set up to preserve the rights of the public in the wood. It relied in the main upon the generosity of the local inhabitants to manage the wood, until it was re-organised in 1979 to allow funding to be obtained from public bodies and local authorities. The committee still manages the wood today and you wilL see more of their signs as the walk progresses. Incidentally, the "Hurt" in Hurtwood is the old name for bilberries, which still grow in abundance in the wood today.*

The path winds through woodland to reach a wide track on to which you should turn left. Continue going gently uphill for approximately a quarter of a mile, ignoring a large crossing track, passing silver birches and conifers on both sides. After passing over a second smaller crossing track, continue for approximately 50 metres to reach a fork, where you should take the wide grass track left. Ignore the first two crossing tracks and continue on with views of Leith Hill on your left, until the track forks again.

Take the left fork, ignoring any joining tracks to reach a stone monument with seating at the top of the hill.

Holmbury Hill Fort 261m/855ft(OS. 104430 Map 187). *The stone monument stands roughly in the centre of Holmbury hill fort. From here there are excellent views across the Surrey Weald to the South Downs. Immediately below you is the village of Ewhurst, to your left (east) Leith Hill and to your right (west) Pitch Hill which is on our route. Holmbury fort is one of several iron age hill forts along the Greensand Ridge. It is believed their main purpose was not for defence from each other, but a combined defence against invaders from northern France. The English Channel at this time being marshland and easily traversed by possible invaders. This form of defence existed right up until the second World War 1939-45, when the British army built similar defences along the North Downs. There is also evidence that the Romans had a settlement on the hill.*

To continue, turn back on yourself and take the bridleway on the left marked with a blue "GW" sign indicating that you are now on the Greensand Way. Ignore the path joining from the right as the path you are on bends and at a fork, turn left keeping to the perimeter of the hill, meeting a post again with a blue "GW" arrow. Follow the direction of the arrow, ignoring a turning right to take the narrow path which winds gently downhill, still following the blue "GW" arrows.

Keep to the perimeter of the hill ignoring all turnings off until you meet

a post with a yellow arrow to descend some steps. Continue up the bank the other side to arrive at a car park. Walk across the car park and out of the main entrance and cross the road to join a footpath ahead of you. There is a good view ahead of the Duke of Kent School, to where we are heading.

The path winds downhill passing through a gate way. At a second farm gate, turn left to walk between fenced fields, following the yellow "GW" sign. Cross over a stile and continue straight on, do not turn right. At the end of the second field, take time to look behind you at the view, particularly the large property, "Coverwood", to the left. Then continue over a ridge ignoring the track on your right and follow the path downhill until it meets a road opposite the gate house to the Duke of Kent School. Cross the road and proceed up the driveway to the school and take the footpath marked on your right to go up wide wooden steps. The path then goes steeply uphill behind the school buildings and crosses another path to continue uphill, still following the yellow "GW" signs.

At a "T" junction, turn left on to a wide track, ignoring all turnings off until you meet a house on your right. Pass the house and take the first small path right, which starts as the perimeter hedge ends. The path goes diagonally uphill occasionally affording good views to your left of Holmbury Hill and Leith Hill beyond. At the top you will meet a "T" junction at which you should turn left on to another wide track. Pass a bench on your left and ignore all turnings off to the right, to follow the perimeter of the hill to the final ridge. Here the path bends sharply right to reach the summit of Pitch Hill (257m), marked by a white stone trig point.

The views from Pitch Hill are once again superb (the best views are gained from a bench just below the path as it bends right to reach the summit). The Surrey Weald stretches out before you to the South Downs, where in clear weather you can see the Chanctonbury Ring a tree covered hill fort. There is still a great deal of woodland in the Weald, the remains of a great impenetrable forest which the Romans called Anderida Silva meaning uninhabited place.

From the trig point continue straight ahead taking the main path going north, to lead down to a car park after passing a quarry on your right. On reaching the car park, cross the road ahead taking the footpath next to a sign for "Mill Cottage".

If you are in need of refreshments turn left along the road to reach "The Windmill" pub (King & Barnes). The pub has a beautiful garden set on the side of a hill, which is extremely pleasant in summer. The menu is somewhat upmarket. Years ago the pub acted as a safe house for smugglers and had a double roof to hide contraband.

To continue our route, follow the path ahead steeply uphill until you reach a junction of tracks with Ewhurst windmill on your left.

Ewhurst Windmill (OS. 077428 Map 187), *is 800 ft above sea level and has been a major landmark for years. It was always a feature on early maps of the area, the earliest recorded windmill on this site dating from 1648. Around 1845 the mill blew down in a gale when the miller failed to turn the sails into the wind. The miller came down with the building but luckily survived. The mill was replaced by the one you can see today but ceased working around 1885. In 1907, after several years of neglect, it was turned into a residence which it continues to be today.*

Take the track past the windmill forking to the left which winds round to "Four Winds Cottage", where you should turn right continuing along a smaller track downhill crossing two drive ways before meeting a road. Cross the road on to another road ahead and then turn left into a car park, still following the signs for the Greensand Way. The footpath bears right out of the car park and soon reaches a clearing which offers more superb views and has a log on which you can rest, known as Lord Justice James Seat. The log can be identified by an inscription dated 1881.

Continue on the path following the perimeter of the hill and when the path forks, turn right. The path continues through woodland and bends left to run parallel with a lane on your right. Go straight on ignoring a crossing path and descend gently until you meet the lane at a clearing, with a gully coming in from your left. Cross the lane to take the public bridleway opposite which is signposted, ignoring the path leading off to the right. You are now leaving the Greensand Way.

Follow the bridleway for a short distance until you meet a bridleway signpost at which you should fork right. The bridleway winds through woodland which is predominantly silver birch and crosses a wide junction of private tracks. At the next junction, cross this to take the bridleway ahead which is signposted, and which turns sharply left almost immediately, to the left of a concrete water tank. Do not take the footpath straight ahead.

The bridleway takes you down through a shallow valley to cross a wide gravel track, still going downhill. Ignore all further crossing tracks and bear left when the path forks at some pylons. Again ignore all crossing tracks and continue along the bottom of the valley to arrive at a house on your right. Follow the driveway ahead, ignoring a path on your right, for approximately 200 metres until you reach a path forking right just before another property. Take this path right to reach a small lane, where you should turn right on to the drive passing through "Lockhurst Hatch Farm". Walk through the farm and go through a farm gate on to an old byway between steep banks.

Continue on passing a footpath on your right and approximately 50 paces further at a fork, take the bridleway right and not the public footpath left. Continue along the bridleway passing between fields with a very large house on the ridge to your left, "Knowle Grange". The path ends at the driveway to "Knowle Grange" and you should continue along this with views of the North Downs on the left, to reach a lane.

Turn left and after 100 metres, turn right on to a signposted public bridleway to pass through a small gate and then veer left down a grass path. Do not make the mistake of taking the driveway ahead.

Continue along the left hand perimeter of the field, pass through a gate and follow the line of another field to pass through another gate and continue along the right hand perimeter of a playing field to meet a road. At the road turn left and after approximately 75 metres, turn right along a signposted public footpath beside "Quakers Orchard".

Continue up the drive passing a rather grand Georgian style house on your right and go straight on ignoring a stile on your left. Follow the left hand perimeter of a field and continue down to Peaslake village. The path comes out at "The Hurtwood Inn", a THF pub and hotel.

Peaslake Village (OS. 087446 Map 187) *lies tucked away from the outside world amongst the lower slopes of Leith Hill. The church built in 1829 is the daughter church of St. James' in Shere. Peaslake has always been associated with Quakers and has a Quaker cemetery situated south of the village. Many of the buildings are made of local stone and so blend neatly with the surrounding hills.*

At the village centre is "The Hurtwood Inn" a hotel named after the wood which encircles the village. The hotel which is THF owned, retains a good local atmosphere. Sandwiches are served from the bar along with Courage beers. There is a restaurant for those wanting more.

Follow the road ahead towards the "Peaslake Village Stores", looking out for the bible on your left! Take the small lane to the right of the stores, Radnor Road, and turn sharp left on to an unmarked footpath going steeply uphill, passing a house on your left, "Brackenside".

This comes out on to a small driveway where it is worth stopping to take a last look back at the village, before continuing straight ahead passing "Tor Cottage" on your left. The path goes between houses and then enters woodland. At a crossing path, go straight across ignoring all other paths.

Soon after you will start to descend into a valley which you should cross, ignoring all turnings, to continue up the other side. The path runs along the side of some fields with a large property in view on your left. It then goes over a crossing track beside an unusual beech tree with an amazing tangle of arms, and continues straight ahead.

You will shortly pass through a shallow valley, do not turn off but again continue straight on and soon after, descend steeply into a small but deeper valley still ignoring all joining and crossing tracks.

As you climb the other side the path snakes round to reach a junction of tracks where you should continue straight on. Do not make the mistake of turning right. This then leads you back to the car park from where the walk commenced.

ACCOMMODATION

The Hurtwood Inn, THF, Peaslake. Tel: 0306 730851

On the walk, the Hurtwood Inn is a friendly relaxed hotel at the centre of village life with resident guests and local inhabitants mixing easily in an unpretentious bar. The surrounding countryside is only paces from the front door allowing for a pleasant evening stroll after the excesses of the evening.

Bulmer Farm, Holmbury St. Mary. Tel: 0306 730210

Half a mile from the walk Bulmer Farm is a lovely 17th century farmhouse offering first class accommodation at very reasonable prices. Guests can enjoy a lovely beamed lounge with log fires in winter and a large well planned garden. Bulmer Farm is in a good location if you wish to attempt the "Holmbury Hurt" and the "Leith Hill Limp" in one weekend.

Youth Hostel, Holmbury St. Mary. Tel: 0306 730777

On the walk, a purpose built youth hostel set in large attractive grounds. The setting is superb, take one step out of the grounds and you are in the extensive Hurtwood. The youth hostel can be busy in summer with school parties - so be warned. Camping is permitted in the grounds

SNAKING THE MOLE

Distance: 10½ miles (17 km)
Time: Allow approximately 5 hours, more if you wish to explore the villages.
Map: Ordnance Survey Landranger Map 187

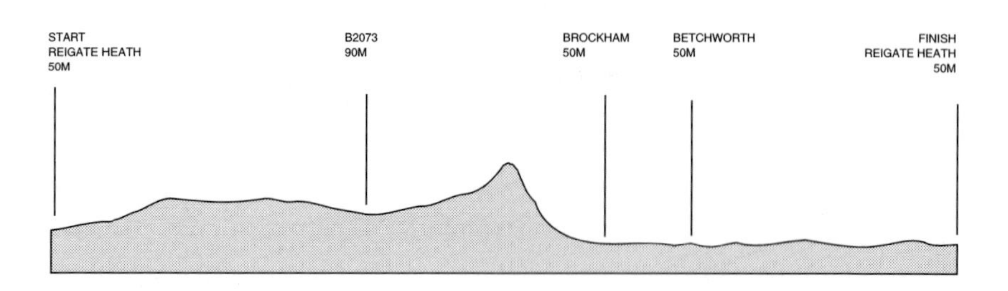

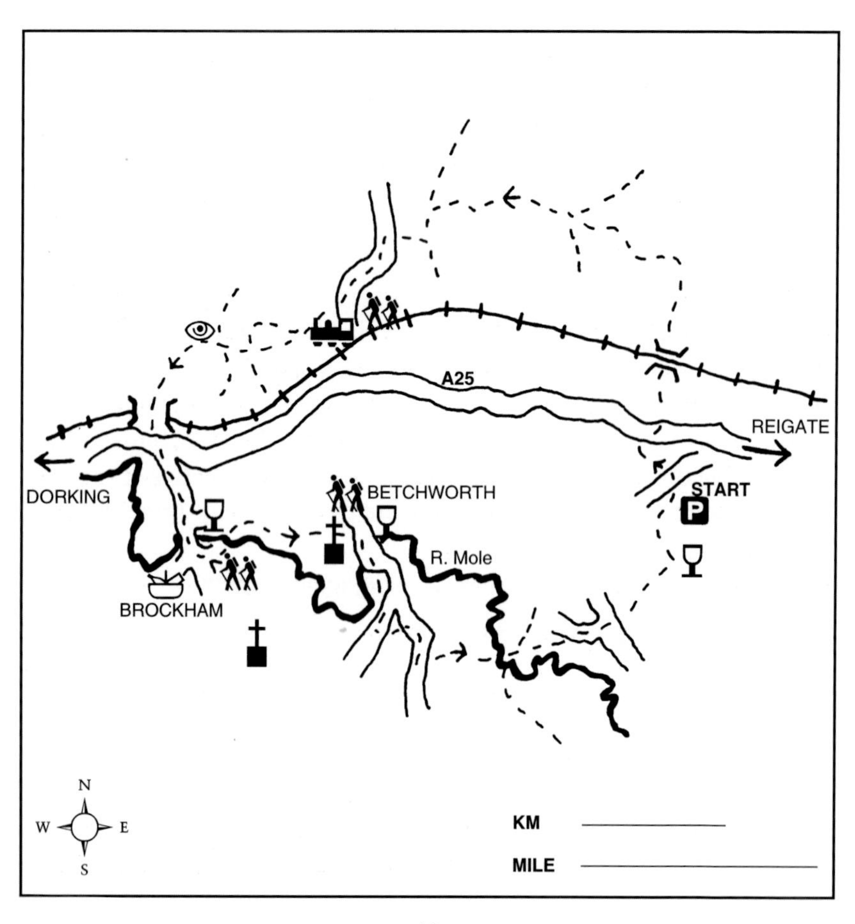

Walk Summary

Snaking the Mole is a walk in the shadow of the North Downs. Apart from one short stretch above Brockham lime works, the walk is low level and therefore fairly easy going. Much of the walk follows close to the course of the river Mole, which you cross no less than four times. Other than the river, there are two other main attractions, Betchworth and Brockham, two of the most picturesque villages in Surrey. One word of warning, walking close to a river invariably means mud and good footwear is essential. In extreme weather parts of the valley can even flood and the route simply becomes impassible. Unless you have a wet suit in your ruck sack, choose your day out with care.

Start - OS. 239503 Map 187

The walk starts from the car park on Reigate Heath, marked with a blue "P" on Ordnance survey map 187. To get there take the turning south beside "The Black Horse" pub off of the A25, just west of Reigate. The car park is the first parking area on the left shortly after passing the last of the cottages on the same side. Other alternative starting points, are Betchworth Railway Station (OS. 210513 Map 187), Brockham village (OS. 197496 Map 187) and Betchworth village (OS. 211498 Map 187). Reigate has a railway station and from there it is only a twenty minute walk to the car park on Reigate Heath.

SNAKING THE MOLE

From the car park, cross the road and take the main footpath behind a wooden post (this could at a later date become a sign) and waste bin travelling in a westerly direction. Do not take the smaller path going diagonally left beside a bench. The path, which is quite prominent, graduates into a grass track passing a golf tee on your left.

To your left you will see a windmill rising proudly out of the Heath. The windmill, which is in excellent condition ceased working many years ago, however it does not lie idle as today it has an equally important role as a church. Continue along the track as it bends north going straight over a crossing track and up a small mound, which is in fact a burial mound topped with scotch pines and a bench. Go down the other side heading for the main road, the A25, to arrive at a small clearing used as a car park.

Cross the A25 and turn right along the road for approximately 50 metres and then left into Clifton Lane, marked as a bridleway. Pass a pretty cottage, "Little Everest", and continue along the lane passing more attractive properties as you go, in particular, "The Old Manor", a fine Wealden farmhouse. After "The Old Manor", open fields allow good views to the west of Betchworth quarry.

Pass under a railway bridge, some metres after which the lane turns sharply left. Leave the lane at this point, to continue ahead passing through a small wooden gate on to a tree lined bridleway with fields either side. The bridleway begins to climb gradually and enters the tree line where you meet a crossing track. Here you should turn left, on to the North Downs Way. Follow the North Downs Way, which is marked by white acorns, along the bottom of Juniper and Buckland hills.

This part of the route is very beautiful and gives a real feeling of isolation. You will pass through woodland and open grass hillside with a patchwork of rambling bushes which include wild rose. In the spring and summer delicate chalkland flowers play host to a beautiful array of butterflies and birds rarely seen in the garden sing as though not a care in the world.

You must keep to the North Downs Way (ensure you follow the white acorn signs) to come out on to a fenced path leading away from the hills between fields. The approximate distance from joining the North Downs Way to this point is one and three quarter miles. At the far end of the fields pass through an iron weighted gate, turning right almost immediately to cross a stile on to a straight path between an avenue of trees. You are still on the North Downs Way.

The path arrives at a main road where you should turn left along the road to cross and join the other side where the pavement ends and begins respectively. Continue along the pavement, which at first is set back from the road behind a line of yew trees, and continue until you reach a lane on your right, The Coombe, into which you should turn. You may have noticed a tudor style house "Cranmer Cottage" on your left. This was built in the early part of the century, the timbers used are meant to have come from the Palace of Archbishop Cranmer.

At a fork, turn left up a gravel lane, passing 1-16 "New Cottages" and carry straight on on a path between fences, again following the white acorn signs. The path crosses a red brick bridge over a chalk quarry and continues through dense undergrowth.

i ***Betchworth Quarries (OS. 206516 Map 187)****. The huge chalk quarries scarring the North Downs at this point are the remains of Betchworth lime works. The works belonged to the Dorking Greystone Lime Company, founded in 1865 by William Finlay, and only ceased trading in 1959. The works had its own railway which joined the main line just west of Betchworth station. The trucks used were originally* *drawn by horses, the first steam locomotive being put into operation in 1871. The land on which the works stand was leased from Sir Benjamin Brodie, the royal surgeon to Queen Victoria, who resided at Broome Park in Betchworth. For almost 100 years, the quarries played a major role in the lives of the people of Betchworth and if you are observant a few relics from this recent past are still visible.*

Ignore all paths going off to the left or right to emerge on to freshly dug chalk. Continue over what is at the time of writing, a bare chalk ridge above a landfill site and go down the other side to re-enter undergrowth and yew trees.

Ignore all joining paths still following the North Downs Way, to reach more open hillside and continue along the left hand bank of a ditch. Go uphill, still ignoring all joining paths, and stay on the path as it runs in and out of the ditch. You will shortly reach a clearing overlooking Brockham lime works on the left with excellent views across to Leith Hill. If you have children make sure they are under control, the sheer drop on the left is over 200 feet.

The path becomes steeper as it goes to reach a turning near the top on the left up some steps, which you should now take. On the right hand side, you will pass a grave stone which is dedicated to a horse. The inscription reads "Memorial to Quick - 29.09.36 to 22.10.44 An English Thoroughbred". Continue along the top of the hill for some distance to turn left on to a path coming in from the right. Continue on and shortly after, pass a tree stump on your right which has been made into a giant chair. The path then begins to go steeply downhill, ignore the stepped path on your right, thereby leaving the North Downs Way.

At a crossing track near the bottom of the hill with a pill box on the left albeit slightly hidden, go straight across to follow the fenced path between fields. Pass over a railway bridge and head for the main road, the A25, which you should cross to join the small road ahead, Brockham Lane, signposted to Brockham. Follow Brockham Lane passing Brockham playing fields on your left and continue between houses to cross over the river Mole by a small bridge.

Ahead of you Brockham village skirts its famous green with Christ Church at its head.

Brockham (OS. 197496 Map 187). *Brockham's most recent claim to fame is that it is host to the biggest Guy Fawkes bonfire in Surrey. Before that it was cricket and many famous names graced the green, including W. G. Grace himself. Apart from the church, Brockham has a less prominent place of worship. On the northern edge of the green is Surrey's* *oldest chapel, built in the late 18th century. Brockham has a "Village Stores" open on Sundays, stocking a wide range of refreshments for the walker and to the north of the green, alongside the chapel, two pubs, "The Royal Oak" and "The Duke's Head", both Friary Meux and serving food.*

Turn left along the green passing in front of the two pubs to reach a white gate with a sign "Brockham Pound Circa. 18th Century". Turn left here along a tarmac public bridleway passing through a smaller white gate. As you go downhill look out for the pond on your right. Cross over the river Mole and turn right to follow a wide bridleway which is marked "GW", indicating you are now on the Greensand Way. This very quickly bends around to the left just before some houses, where you should leave the main bridleway to take the path on the right, marked as a public footpath and "GW".

Follow this with houses on your left and the river Mole as it snakes along on the right. Pass through some iron bars into a field and continue to pass through more iron bars, keeping to the right hand perimeter with goods views on your left of the North Downs and Betchworth quarry.

Continue on passing horse chestnut trees to a corner of the field. Pass through two wooden posts on to a fenced path directly ahead which runs between trees and a field on your left, heading for farm buildings. This is still the Greensand Way. Cross over a concrete drive passing through gates either side and follow the path to pass a car park on your left and enter St. Michael's church yard through a small wooden gate. You are now at Betchworth.

Betchworth (OS. 211498 Map 187)*, another Surrey village which transports you back in time situated on the north bank of the river Mole, has one of the best collections of 17th century properties in the county. Much earlier, there was a castle but this fell into ruin during the reign of Queen Anne and has now disappeared. Betchworth is unique in that over the centuries, three of its doctors have been medical advisors to the royal family. Thomas Morsted, doctor to Henry IV, V and VI (obviously a survivor!). Sir Benjamin Brodie, surgeon to Queen Victoria and more recently, Sir Dyce Duckworth. Memorials to all three doctors' families can be found in Betchworth church. The church is originally Saxon, though much rebuilding has all but hidden its roots. However, it remains a very attractive building and nestles comfortably between "Betchworth House", the 17th century manor and the village forge housed in cottages from the same period. There are many other buildings* *of note at Betchworth, but perhaps to the walker the most important is "The Dolphin Inn", another fine 17th century building and one of the last inns in Surrey to brew its own ale. It is now a Youngs pub still serving fine ales but does not serve food.*

Walk through the church yard noting the very old head stones, some made out of wood. One of particular interest is the grave of Clara and William Judd. William Judd was the captain of the bell ringers at St. Michael's for thirty six years around the turn of the century. The grave stone, which is on the left just past the main entrance to the church, is appropriately decorated with three bells.

Leave the church yard through an archway passing "Forge Cottage" on your left and an entrance to "Betchworth House" on your right. The village pub "The Dolphin", is on your left. Turn right along the grass verge above the road following the perimeter of Betchworth House, cross over the river Mole for the third time and shortly after, turn right over a stile on to a well kept footpath across a field. There are good views across the river of Betchworth House. At the other side of the field follow the path to enter some trees. Cross over a stile and continue uphill to cross a second stile into a field. Follow the field along the right hand perimeter until it opens out on your right, sweeping down to meet the river Mole.

The scenery here is particularly pretty with ducks often frequenting the river below. Turn left at this point crossing the field to go over a stile on to a narrow lane. Cross the lane and the stile directly ahead into another field and go diagonally left across the field to a stile. Go over the stile and immediately after, a narrow footbridge and continue along the right hand side of the field, taking in more good views on your left of the North Downs and Betchworth quarry as well as views to the south.

Cross a stile into a lane and turn right to follow the lane, passing "Snowerhill Farm", for approximately a quarter of a mile turning left at a public footpath sign to pass through an iron gate. Head towards a gate way in the left hand corner of the field, ignoring the gate on the immediate left.

Pass through the gate way and go straight on through the next field following a line of oak trees to a gap into the field ahead. Continue straight on passing a line of trees on your right and a footpath sign on your left with good views ahead of Reigate Hill. At the second footpath sign, turn right and follow this in a southerly direction. Behind the footpath sign is a lovely but disused house.

Follow the line of trees to the bushes ahead. Do not go left before the bushes but pass them to turn left immediately after at a small wooden post marked with a yellow arrow. Keep left to cross the field ahead, keeping to the left hand perimeter. Pass through some wooden posts to enter a copse and shortly after cross the river Mole for the last time, by way of the concrete bridge.

Continue straight on, ignoring the path on the left. Pass a pill box and leave the main path crossing a stile ahead into a field. Go across the field, passing a second pill box on your left with the river on your right as the field gradually narrows. This is a lovely place on a sunny day to take time for a rest.

After following the river Mole all this time you may wonder how the river got its name. No-one is sure though it is most probably named after the mole, the animal, which has made its home along the worm rich banks.

At the next pill box cross the stile on your left into a field and turn right to follow the perimeter of the field to a lane, with a large house directly ahead of you, "Trumpets Hill". Turn right along the lane, which is a bridleway, passing a farm house on your right, to meet another lane.

There are good views again on your left of the North Downs. Cross the lane and go straight on along a fenced and signposted public footpath, passing "Littleton Nursing Home" on the left. Cross a stile and go across the field over another stile to join a wooden fenced track ahead, heading for a farmhouse, "Littleton Manor Farm". It is hard to believe that the wooded hill ahead of you is Reigate's Priory Park backing on to a busy shopping street.

Pass to the left of the farmhouse on to the drive way and as this bends right towards a pond, leave the drive way to cross a stile ahead.

Continue along the path bending round to the right in front of some farm buildings and then left to rejoin the tarmac drive. As the drive bends right again, turn left on to a bridleway. Do not cross the stile into the field but follow the bridleway which is signposted to Reigate Heath, uphill between steep banks. The bridleway soon peaks and descends to arrive at "The Skimmington Castle" pub (Friary Meux). The Skimmington Castle, despite its recently built out of place car park, remains one of the oldest and best pubs in Surrey. The bar is filled with a collection of pipes. The loosely matched furniture would grace any antique shop and if you are not happy to just mellow, there is an unusual version of "hoopla" to capture your interest. The pub serves basic food.

Follow the bridleway to the right of the pub on to the lane leading from the pub. Another lane quickly joins from the right from some cottages, and just after you should turn right on to a prominent track. This passes a golf green on your left just after which you should turn left on to a narrow path heading for some trees passing tee 16 on your right. Continue on through Reigate Heath until you reach the car park from where our walk commenced.

ACCOMMODATION

Cranleigh Hotel, Reigate. Tel: 0737 223417

Half a mile from the walk, the Cranleigh Hotel is a smart friendly hotel, complete with attractive gardens and heated open air swimming pool.

White Horse Hotel (THF), Dorking. Tel: 0306 881138

Two miles from the walk, the hotel has a good restaurant and comfortable rooms, especially in the older parts of the building. At the rear is a secluded open air heated swimming pool.

Youth Hostel, Tanners Hatch YHA, Polesden Lacey, Dorking. Tel: 0372 52528

Five miles from the walk, Tanners Hatch is an isolated cottage (you can only reach it by foot). Situated in the woods of Ranmore Common, the hostel has no electricity so bring your own lighting. Camping is also permitted.

Camping, Polesden Lacey, Dorking. Tel: 0372 456844

Five miles from the walk, this is a Camping and Caravanning Club site in a beautiful setting on an old cricket pitch in the grounds of Polesden Lacey, N.T. Please note, that only tents and trailer tents are permitted.

N.B. Dorking and Reigate have a wide choice of accommodation. Contact Surrey County Council's Leisure and Tourism Unit, Kingston Upon Thames, KT1 2DN, for a free booklet

BATTING THE BUCK

Distance: 11½ miles (18.5 km)

Time: Allow approximately 6 hours, more if possible.

Map: Ordnance Survey Landranger Map 186

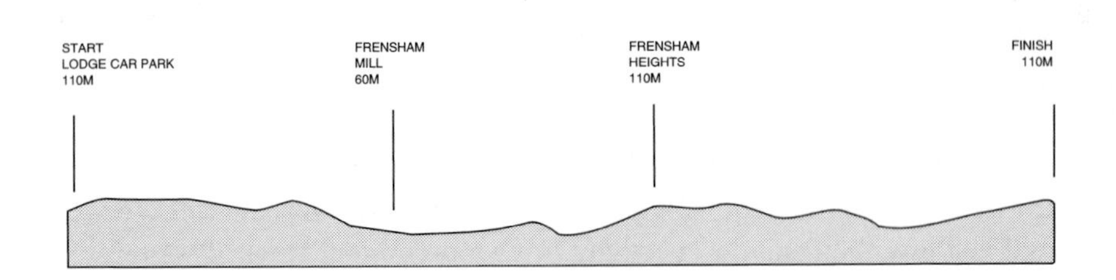

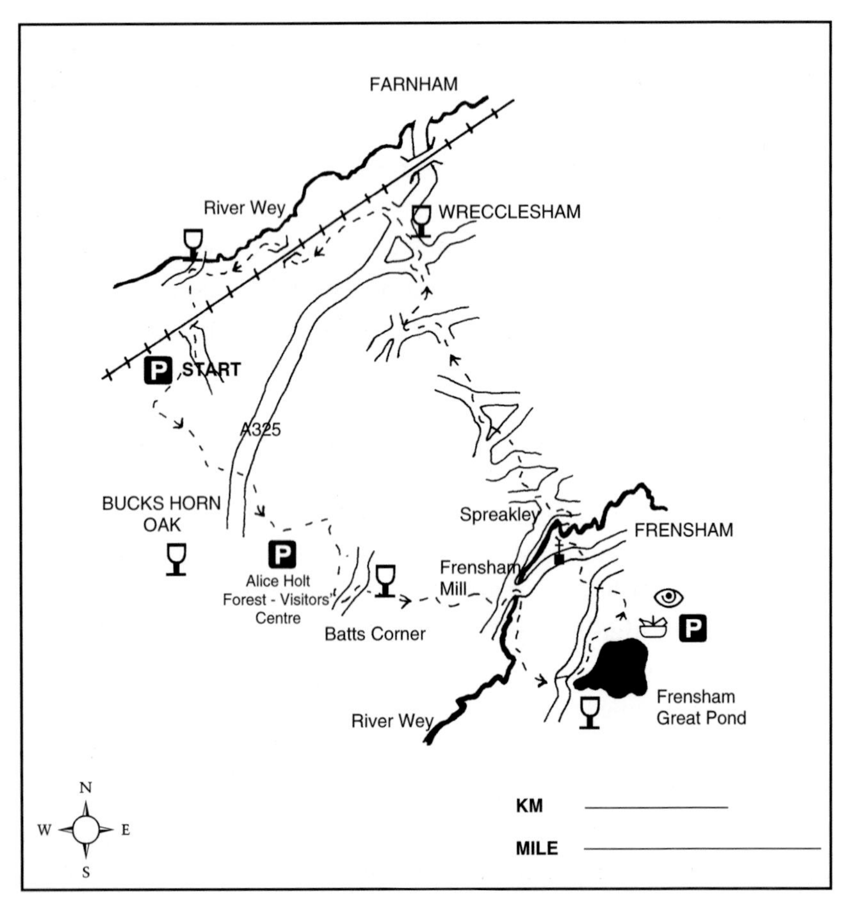

Walk Summary

Batting the Buck is a walk with a wealth of content. You are never far from water (which means the going can become very muddy) and will be delighted by the beauty that it has to offer. The walk also passes many buildings of interest and although being a lowland walk, will often surprise with some beautiful views. The danger is, there is so much to see that you will forget the time and end up as I once did feeling your way back to the start in the dark. I recommend an early start to get the full benefit.

Start - OS. 803434 Map 186

The walk starts from the entrance to the Lodge Enclosure car park and picnic area of Alice Holt forest. This is situated on a lane that passes Alice Holt Lodge, a Forestry Commission research station (signposted) between the A325 near Bucks Horn Oak and the A31. Other easy places to start the walk are the Alice Holt forest visitor centre (OS. 811417 Map 186) or the car park at Frensham Great Pond (OS. 844403 Map 186). Farnham has a railway station which is two miles from the walk along the A31.

BATTING THE BUCK

From the entrance to the car park walk along the main track passing a small parking and picnic area on your left and later the sign for the Arboretum Walk and the main car park on your right. Ignore a wide track on your left and continue straight on until you reach a tarmac drive.

Turn left along the tarmac drive, following the signs for Alice Holt research station and passing a fenced pond on your right. As you continue along the drive, you will pass an avenue of houses and the research centre, a large stately property on your left.

As the drive turns left towards the research centre, turn right instead on to a track and continue until you reach a crossroad of tracks, where you should turn left passing an open field on your right to reach the main road, the A325.

Cross the road and go straight along the track ahead for about 40 paces which then bends left. Stay on this track and turn first right, almost going back on yourself, to continue along a well used track ignoring all other tracks until you reach a signposted coach park on your left. To visit the Alice Holt visitor centre continue straight on and you will see the centre ahead on the left.

Alice Holt Forest and Visitor Centre (OS. 811417 Map 186). *Alice Holt forest is managed by the Forestry Commission and is a popular recreation area for the inhabitants of nearby Farnham and Guildford. The careful management of the forest, which is a pleasant mixture of broadleaf and coniferous trees, has enabled the wildlife to live comfortably with the minimum of disturbance from man. The forest boasts a herd of Roe deer of about 120, although this is a considerable drop from the 18th century when the herd numbered 800. The herd then would have been a mixture of Fallow and Red deer as well as the Roe. The forest also supports a wealth of smaller mammals. Birds, butterflies and moths are equally at home. The important thing is to be constantly alert and you will reap the benefits the forest has to offer. The visitor centre provides more detailed information about the forest and its walks and also sells souvenirs to remember your visit. Of particular interest are some excellent wood carvings for which a local forester is famous. Please note that the taking of flora and fauna from the forest is strictly forbidden without a permit.*

To continue our walk, turn left immediately after the coach park and follow a grass track running between an avenue of trees. Ignore the first crossing track and any minor joining tracks. At the second crossing track turn right on to a gravel track gently descending, to bear left at a fork and follow the gravel track downhill ignoring a large track joining from the left. Continue downhill, ignoring a narrow gravel path on your right and shortly after bear left when the track forks. Take the next turning left which is a smaller gravel path. Follow this for a short distance until the path turns sharply left at which point you should turn off and continue straight ahead along a narrow now ungravelled path heading towards some tall pines.

The path meets the pines and bears right. Continue along the path until you reach a small fork where you should bear left over a very small sometimes hidden stream. Go uphill to reach the top where it is worth looking back at the view of Alice Holt forest. The path bends round to the right and on your left you will see some houses, the second of which is a converted chapel. At this point, turn left along a small path which leads out onto a road to the right of the chapel. Turn left along the road to the green where you will find "The Blue Bell" pub, a freehouse.

Bats Corner and Dockenfield (OS. 820410). *You arrive at Bats Corner beside a non-conformist chapel, now a private residence. The village is spread out, the centre being a street of houses with large gardens. The true heart of the village is its pub, "The Blue Bell", which* *dates from the 16th century and was once the village bakery. It still has the original ovens. The pub stocks an excellent range of beers and serves good food, which makes it, in my opinion, one of the best pubs in Surrey. At the bottom of the hill a short walk from Bats Corner, lies Dockenfield famed for once being the home of the founder of the Boy Scout movement, Lord Baden Powell.*

Turn right to pass in front of the pub and go downhill along the lane which becomes a bridleway. The bridleway is marked by blue topped posts. There is open common land on your right, beyond which the roof tops of Dockenfield nestle comfortably in the valley below. The bridleway becomes a lane once again and you continue between attractive properties, passing a pond on your right leaving the lane as it bears right, to go straight on passing a house called "Orchard End" on your left.

The bridleway ahead continues between fenced fields for approximately three quarters of a mile until it meets a road with a cottage on your right. "Frensham Manor" can be seen directly ahead between trees and looking to your left, you will see two oast houses. These are a reminder that this part of the Wey valley supported a thriving hop growing industry which once served the local breweries of Alton and Farnham. At the road turn left and then first right passing a white cottage and suddenly a piece of forgotten England opens out in front of you.

"Frensham Mill" (OS. 836410 Map 186) *is a wonderfully pleasant surprise. The mill pond on your left bubbles and froths as the waters cascading over the mill race hit it with force. The road curves gently to pass over the race in front of an elegant brick mill house. A mill has stood on this site since at least the early 13th century. Unfortunately, the milling ceased in 1920 and the mill was demolished two years later, with the exception of the mill house and granary. The mill house is in excellent condition and its beauty makes you wonder how it could ever have been an industrial building. The mill pond and the valley through which you will shortly pass, supports a dazzling variety of water loving plants as well as birds such as sandmartins and kingfishers, keep your eyes peeled.*

Turn right into the "Mill House" courtyard and join the bridleway running adjacent to the property. Continue uphill to pass "Frensham Manor" on your left which is almost completely hidden from view by its high perimeter wall. From here follow the bridleway which in turn follows the river all the way to Frensham Great Pond.

On the way you will pass a beautiful tranquil pond, frequented by fishermen and at one point the path will fork, either path is acceptable as they rejoin later. The bridleway emerges at a road with Frensham Great Pond ahead of you.

On your right you will see "The Frensham Pond Hotel". However, unless you are in need of refreshment, turn left to follow the road along the edge of the pond until you see a track on your right marked by a blue topped post. The track continues to skirt the pond with views across to "The Frensham Pond Hotel" and sailing club.

i ***Frensham Great Pond (OS. 845403 Map 186)*** *is a natural spring fed pond enlarged by man. It was originally used in the early 13th century to provide the Bishop of Winchester with fresh fish at his castle in Farnham. The Great Pond is actually the largest of a chain of three ponds, the next pond, Little Pond, also provided fish for the Bishop. The smallest pond, Abbot's Pond, provided fish for the monks at Waverley Abbey. The waterside garden of "The Frensham Pond Hotel" has been designed around a series of tiny pools, which were once "stew ponds" and were used to spawn the fish. In 1913 the first sea plane was tested on the pond. Then, years later during the second World War, the pond was drained to avoid being a directional aid to another plane, the enemy bomber. The best time to see the ponds is early morning, when you can watch the birds through the morning mist in search of the first meal of the day.*

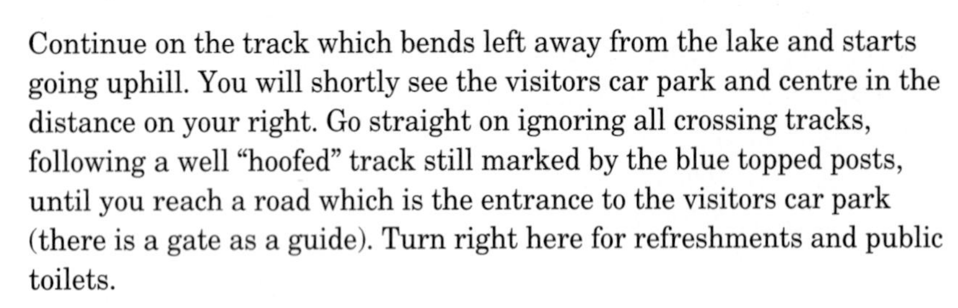

Continue on the track which bends left away from the lake and starts going uphill. You will shortly see the visitors car park and centre in the distance on your right. Go straight on ignoring all crossing tracks, following a well "hoofed" track still marked by the blue topped posts, until you reach a road which is the entrance to the visitors car park (there is a gate as a guide). Turn right here for refreshments and public toilets.

To continue our route, cross the road and join bridleway 45, also marked "no vehicles", to go uphill, ignoring a crossing track. At the next crossing track turn left and continue to the top of the hill to take in the superb view behind you of Frensham Great Pond. Carry straight on over the heather crested hill top and follow the path as it bends sharply to the right, passing a large dead tree on your left.

Just after this you will see a very small footpath on your left (this can be easily missed - if you reach a wide crossing track you have gone too far and should retrace your steps).

Take the small path between gorse bushes until you reach a road at the bottom of the hill. Cross the road, turn left and approximately 30 paces on, turn right on to a signposted footpath. This comes out at a small residential road which you should cross to join the path ahead, passing a park on your left to arrive at some small cottages. Continue ahead to the end of the cottages, the last being "The Toll House", where you turn left into Frensham Village with St. Mary's church ahead.

Frensham Village and church (OS. 844413 Map 186). *Frensham is an attractive village often overshadowed by its famous ponds. The church dates from the 13th century, when it was moved to its present site. The reason for its move and its original site remain a mystery, but it is known that the area suffered severe flooding in the mid-13th century. The abbey four miles down stream flooded to a depth of eight feet and if the original site of the church was nearer the river, this could explain its move. The squat but sturdy tower is 14th century and houses eight bells. If you visit the church, look for the large beaten copper caldron. Its most likely use was for church ales in the Middle Ages, though there are stories that it came from the kitchens of Waverley Abbey and even a tale that it belonged to Mother Ludlam, the Waverley witch. One pleasant association with Frensham, is the "Frensham Rose" a once popular rose of rich red flowers and glossy green foliage. The rose was created by crossing "Crimson Glory" with an un-named seedling.*

Cross the road and take the tarmac footpath to the right of the church yard going downhill, shortly bending round to the right to meet up with the river Wey again on your left. Cross the river going over a small wooden hump back bridge and continue uphill. At the top of the hill the path meets a narrow lane. Ignoring the footpath signs, turn left and continue along the lane to the end passing "The Malt House", the name being a clue to its past and "St. Austins" on your left. Turn right along a wider road for approximately 100 metres.

After "Speakley House" which is on your right, turn left into the road opposite "South Cottage" and after a short distance, turn right on to the public footpath opposite the entrance to "Daws Wood" to cross a field diagonally to your left. The grand building on the hill ahead of you is "Frensham Heights School".

At the other side of the field, cross a bridge over a small brook and continue uphill through trees crossing over a stile. Carry straight on with scotch pines on your right, passing through a kissing gate to cross a small lane. Follow the steep sided footpath on the other side uphill, shortly crossing another lane and continue on the footpath to the next lane where you should turn right. The lane takes you to the top of the hill which offers good views to the south.

You soon pass "Frensham Heights school" on your left to continue along the lane until you reach a main road. Cross the road joining the public bridleway ahead of you, ignoring a footpath on your right and continue on taking the left fork on to a narrow path shortly after. As a guide there should be iron railings and rhododendron bushes on your right.

Go straight on passing a lane ending on your left soon after which you will descend steeply to the bottom of a valley, to see a large white house ahead to your left. The path proceeds uphill to lead naturally into Switchback Lane. Carry straight on across a small crossroads into Shrubbs Lane until you reach the main road. Turn left along the road and continue for approximately a quarter of a mile, passing houses on both sides until you reach a slightly hidden footpath on your right next to a bus stop. Take this path signposted Browns Walk, to continue down the side of a valley which allows pleasant views to your left.

The path meets a house at the bottom, turn right here following a stream on your left and after approximately 50 metres, turn left in the direction of a footpath sign to cross over the stream. Follow the path uphill which near the top becomes a track before meeting a road. Turn right along the road and then first left into Pottery Lane, which begins as a pot-holed track and progresses into a tarmac road. Stay on Pottery Lane where after a short while you will see a long brick building with a tiled arch doorway on your left, this is a pottery.

A. Harris & Sons Pottery (OS. 825446 Map 186). *This unique pottery is one of the oldest of its kind in the county. It was founded in 1873 by Absolom Harris on its present site, Clay Hill, the clay being the obvious incentive. Today, the process remains exactly as it was in Absolom's time and a tour around this unique piece of working history is a must. You may even find a suitable souvenir to remember your day out.*

Pottery Lane winds down to join another road, Queenels Hill, into which you should turn right and follow to the bottom and the main road, Wrecclesham Hill. Turn right at the main road and continue to "The Royal Oak" pub, a Morland pub which also offers food and B&B.

At the pub cross the road and take the footpath opposite (Westfield Lane). Follow this downhill, ignoring a marked footpath on the left. At Farnham Mini Rugby Club, you should join a track which bends left following the perimeter of a rugby pitch. At the end of the pitch the track bends right and becomes a fenced path leading through a landfill site. Take note of the "No Smoking" signs or you could be viewing your route from the air!

Turn left when the path meets a railway line and continue to an arch under the railway on your right. The path under the arch leads across fields to "Willey Mill", a trout farm which also rears rare pigs as well as selling a small selection of groceries. Across the main road beyond, the A31, is the entrance to the Trevena House Hotel (recommended accommodation). If you are not staying at the hotel and do not require refreshments, ignore the railway arch and continue straight on following the path with the railway on your right and a large quarry on your left.

I make no excuse for taking you through this unusual, some would say unpleasant, landscape. The quarry can be as much magnificent as it is ugly and is an important part of our industrial heritage as are the oast and mill houses passed earlier on the walk.

Go over a stile into woodland, predominantly made up of oak and sweet chestnut trees and continue to cross another stile into a field. Keep to the perimeter of the field, still with the railway line on your right and after passing through a kissing gate, turn right to pass under the railway. After passing through the arch turn immediately left crossing a stile into a field. On your right you will once again see the river Wey and beyond, the A31.

Keep to the left hand perimeter of the field, at the end of which you should turn right and go down into the woods to join the small footpath beside the river. Cross over a stile and follow the path up river, crossing a small stream and thereafter another stile. Follow the river bank to a third stile which you should cross and continue to the end of the field. Do not leave the field but turn left at the road in front of a house, in the direction of the footpath sign. Go uphill across a large open field to meet a very small reed covered stream. As a rough guide, head to the left of an oak tree in the middle of the field.

Keep the small stream, sometimes dry, on your left and continue up into the woods, crossing the railway line in front of you. Follow the path ahead through trees meeting a wider track joining from the left and continue straight ahead until you meet a road. Join the road and continue straight on (do not turn right), to reach the Lodge Enclosure car park and the start of our walk.

ACCOMMODATION

Frensham Pond Hotel, Frensham Great Pond. Tel: 025125 5161

On the walk, this is the place to stay if you want to treat yourself. Originally 15th century, the hotel which has been extensively modernised has excellent views across Frensham Great Pond.

Trevena House Hotel, Alton Road, Nr. Farnham. Tel: 0252 716908

Half a mile from the walk, the Trevena House Hotel is a Victorian manor house in gothic style with an excellent oak panelled and tartan entrance hall. Complete with outdoor swimming pool and tennis court, this very relaxed hotel is excellent value for money.

Youth Hostel, Hindhead YHA, Devils Punchbowl, Hindhead. Tel: 0428 734285

Seven miles from the walk, a simple youth hostel situated in the bowl of the Devils Punchbowl. Basic but idyllic and I loved it. Camping is also permitted.

Camping and Caravans, Tilford Touring, Tilford. Tel: 025125 3296

Four miles from the walk, the site is in a particularly nice setting surrounded by Hankley Common, within walking distance of the Duke of Cambridge pub. The site is open all year.

BOX HILL BONESHAKER

Distance: 11½ miles (18.5 km)

Time: Allow approximately 5½ hours

Map: Ordnance Survey Landranger Map 187

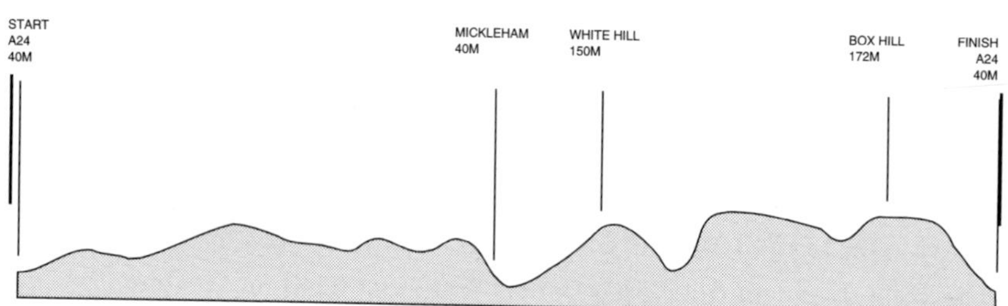

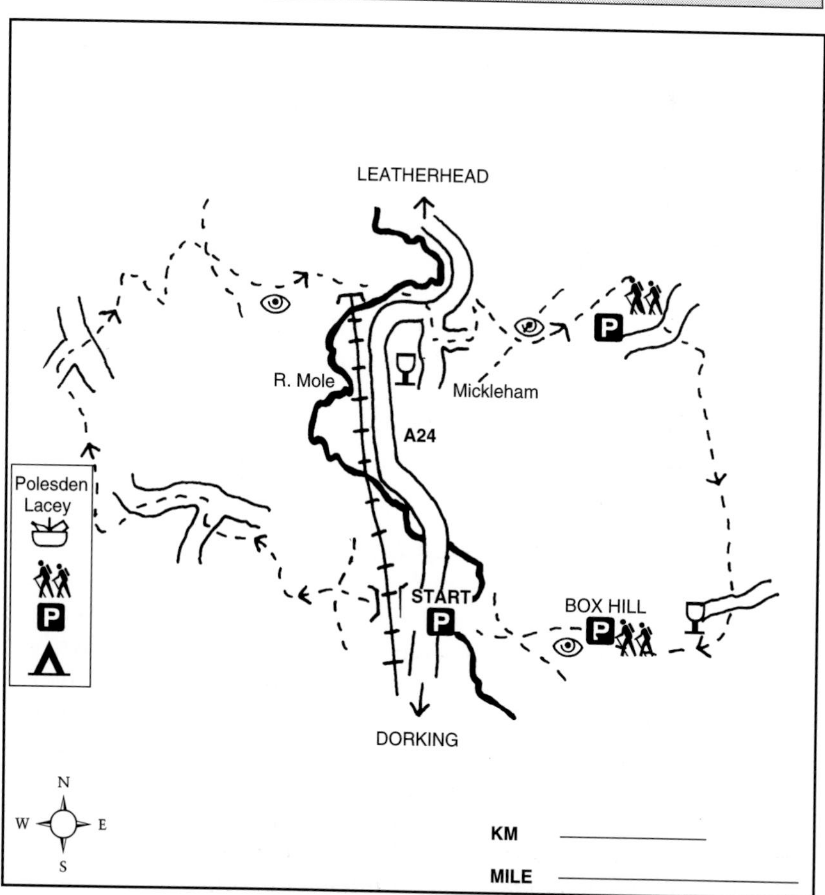

Walk Summary

The Box Hill Bone Shaker explores the hills north of Dorking either side of the river Mole, known locally as the Mole Gap. The several climbs involved will reward the walker with fine views making the effort more than worthwhile. For those interested in architecture, the walk passes close to two magnificent country houses, "Polesden Lacey" (N.T.) and "Norbury House". The walk also follows in the footsteps of two great female novelists, Jane Austen and Fanny Burney, who fell in love with the beauty of the area and honoured it by basing stories around it.

This walk is not for the unfit, the climbs may not be steep but they are persistent and can take their toll on the unwary. Several parts can be slippery so good footwear is essential.

Start - OS. 171513 Map 187

The walk starts on the North Downs Way, just north of Denbies vineyard on the western side of the A24. Though parking is tolerated on the verge here it is best to park in the parking area on the eastern side off the southbound carriageway. This parking area is for people wishing to visit The Stepping Stones and is marked by a small National Trust sign, the entrance being a bus stop.

Other suggested starting points are Polesden Lacey (OS. 137525 Map 187) albeit you will have to pay if you are not a member of the National Trust. Cockshott Wood car park below White Hill (OS. 189536 Map 187) or the car park at the top of Box Hill itself (OS. 179512 Map 187). Dorking has two railway stations close to the start on the A24, Dorking and Dorking Deepdene. There is also a station at West Humble.

THE BOX HILL BONE SHAKER

Before you start the walk you may want to visit the Denbies vineyard which is visible on the left.

i ***Denbies Estate (OS. 165512 Map 187)*** *is currently the largest vineyard in England. It was started in 1986, with the last of the vines being planted in 1990 to cover a total area of 250 acres. There was a vineyard on this site as far back as Roman times, the Romans expertly recognising the value of the south facing slopes and chalky soil, widely regarded as the essential combination for quality wines. "Denbies House" is situated on the North Downs overlooking the estate. The current house is a clever conversion of the laundry to the original house, sadly demolished in 1953. The original house was built by Thomas Cubitt who amongst his achievements, designed Osborne House for Queen Victoria on the Isle of Wight and the old eastern front of Buckingham Palace.*

Prince Albert visited the estate in 1851, planting several rare conifers one of which fell during the storm of 1990 and when I visited, several well turned souvenirs from its wood were on sale. George Cubitt inherited the estate on his father's death and it was he who built the church of St. Barnabas, now also known as "the church on the North Downs Way". Its spire is a landmark which can be seen for miles. The estate passed out of the Cubitt family when it was purchased in 1984 by Adrian White, a Dorking based businessman. The vineyard is Mr. White's brainchild and I for one take my hat off to him. If it's a pleasant day why not visit and purchase a bottle to enjoy later on your walk whilst savouring one of the many excellent views. It comes personally recommended!

If the vineyard doesn't appeal to you or you feel it is safer to visit after the walk, take the wide track west from the A24, signposted as the North Downs Way, to pass under a railway bridge and then a cottage on your left. Go through a wooden gate continuing up a semi tarmacced track with fields to your right and the vineyard on your left. Behind you is the western cliff of Box Hill. Ignore a crossing track and continue uphill for a quarter of a mile to reach a wide track, signposted as a public footpath, on your right in front of some laurel bushes, on to which you should turn right. It's worth spending some moments first however, to look back on your route and a particularly good view of the vineyard.

The track comes out on to a drive way leading to two houses visible above you, "Ashleigh Grange" and "Ashcombe". Turn right here and after the fencing on your left ends, take a narrow sometimes concealed footpath immediately left through bushes. A short detour (quarter of a mile) downhill to the end of the drive leads to West Humble chapel (N.T.) and "Chapel Farm".

i

West Humble Chapel and Chapel Farm (OS. 160519 Map 187).
West Humble chapel now in ruins and in the care of the National Trust, was founded in the 12th century. It had a short life and by the late middle ages ceased to be of any use. Chapel Farm opposite the chapel is open to the public in summer and is well worth a visit especially for families. The farmer gives a "fun ride" around the farm in a trailer which children love.

Staying on our route, the path runs between bushes for about 20 paces to meet a crossing path in front of a stile. Go over the stile and cross a field following the wooden telegraph poles and once over the brow of the hill, head for a metal farm gate beside which is a stile with a yellow arrow. There are good views here of the surrounding countryside and the village below, West Humble. Cross the stile and continue along a narrow footpath, fenced on the right and wooded on the left. This goes slowly down the side of the hill passing through an unusual stile and continues straight on along the right hand perimeter of a field. At the end of the field with cottages on your right, go through a gate and turn right along the lane. At the "T" junction turn left towards Polesden Lacey and Bookham.

The long field to the right of this lane is host to sheep dog trials in summer. Go along the lane for almost half a mile and take the turning on your left beside a gatehouse. Cross a stile beside a large white gate and follow the signs to Polesden Lacey and the Youth Hostel. There is a money box in the wall on the right where payment should be made if you are not a member of the National Trust and wish to visit the grounds at "Polesden Lacey".

Continue straight on along a wide track passing a turning on the left to the youth hostel (YHA) and follow the track as it bends left to meet a small ornate bridge. Do not cross the bridge but turn right to go down some steps and continue along another track uphill. Should you wish to visit "Polesden Lacey" itself, then continue over the bridge.

Polesden Lacey (OS. 136523 Map 187) *is a large early 19th century regency villa now in the care of the National Trust. The current house is one of several which have existed on this site. Joseph Bonsor founder of the present house, was also responsible for planting twenty thousand trees on the estate and much of the beauty of the surrounding countryside must be attributed to him. It is the final owner, the Hon. Mrs. Ronald Greville DBE, the famous socialite of the 1900's, that makes Polesden Lacey so appealing. Mrs. Greville and Polesden Lacey regularly entertained royalty, politicians and other notable socialites for almost forty years. Her parties were legendary and today wandering through the rooms of this great house, the presence of the lady and her guests can still be felt. Indeed, I have often thought that if walls could talk then the walls of this house would certainly be worth listening to. The gardens are magnificent especially the sweeping lawn in front of the house which has beautiful views over Ranmore common. The property has a pleasant restaurant housed in the old stables and a National Trust shop selling a wide range of souvenirs.*

Our route continues uphill through woodland. You will soon pass a gate with a "Camping Club" sign on your left, which leads to the old Polesden Lacey cricket pitch now a camp site and open to Camping and Caravan Club members only (see accommodation). After half a mile the track reaches a lane which is the main drive way to "Polesden Lacey". Cross the lane and turn immediately right on to a wide track running parallel with the lane between beech trees. The houses you can see on your left at this point are the outskirts of Great Bookham.

Great Bookham (OS. 135545 Map 187), *despite its urban sprawl still maintains some character. The rector of the church from 1769 to 1820, the Reverend Samuel Cooke, was godfather to Jane Austen and much of the countryside through which you are currently walking, was used by Jane in her writing. Another great novelist, Fanny Burney, lived here before moving to West Humble. Fanny Burney wrote Camilla whilst living in Great Bookham and it is from this book that Jane Austen found the title for her book, Pride and Prejudice.*

Cross another road at a "T" junction and continue straight ahead along a wide track between hedgerows and fields. After approximately half a mile you will reach a junction of tracks near some houses, turn right on to another track to cross fields going away from the houses heading for some trees. As you enter the trees you will pass a Surrey County Council sign "Norbury Park" and a footpath on your left. Do not turn off but continue straight on along the edge of a field with woodland on your right.

On a clear day you can see on your left Leatherhead and sometimes London with the Nat West and Post Office towers. Pass a gate with a sign, Bookham Wood, on your right and continue until you reach a junction of tracks at the end of the field. Turn left and left again almost going back on yourself walking along the bottom of the field. The track continues to a cottage, "Roaring House Farm", where you should turn right and take the narrow path going uphill signposted as a bridleway.

Pass over a crossing path at the top of the hill and continue straight on going downhill. Go straight over a wide crossing track at the bottom and continue up the other side passing a bench on your left. The path goes slowly uphill through young oaks and later passes a one bar gate on your left with a sign, Fetcham Downs.

The path soon becomes a track and passes through a one bar gate where you should turn left on to a wider track, to reach a triangular junction with picnic tables in the centre. Go straight on do not turn right, passing to the left of the picnic tables to join a tarmac drive. Proceed downhill along the drive past the gates to "Norbury Park", following the boundary fencing.

Norbury Park (OS. 160538 Map 187) *sitting high above the Mole Gap, is an excellently preserved mansion from the 18th century. Norbury Park as it is today was built by George Lock in 1774 and is famous for its Landscape Room, a room decorated with a continuous landscape creating the illusion that you are outdoors. The name Norbury comes* *from the Norbury family who owned the estate for several generations from the 14th to 16th century.*

Norbury Park

As the boundary fencing turns right leading away from the lane, you should should do the same following the fencing along a marked bridleway. Go straight over a drive in front of another set of gates to the house and continue until the bridleway bends left. At this point to your right is a narrow path signposted "View Point". In the summer the sign is hidden in the undergrowth so be careful not to miss it. This path leads to a ridge with spectacular views over the Mole Gap. It is a good place to stop for a rest and a bite to eat or perhaps even to test that bottle of wine from Denbies vineyard. The sweep of woodland ahead to your right is known as Druids Grove.

Rejoin the bridleway from the view point and go steeply downhill, to pass through a grass clearing where there are good views to the other side of the valley. The bridleway eventually joins a tarmac drive. You continue straight down passing an old cedar tree to join and continue down another tarmac drive coming in from the left. Ahead to your left in the valley is Mickleham Priory. Leave the drive as it bends left to join a marked bridleway on your right. Ignore a path coming in from the right as you continue downhill between fences. The bridleway rejoins the tarmac drive where you should turn right to go over the river Mole. Cross the main road, the A24, with care and go up the small road directly ahead to Mickleham.

i

Mickleham (OS. 171535 Map 187) *a village of well kept houses has many notable associations. "Juniper Hall", a fine 18th century house, now a National Trust field studies centre, was once used as a safe house for aristocratic refugees from the French Revolution. General d'Arblay, one of the refugees met Fanny Burney here and later married her at Mickleham church in 1793. Also married at the church was George Meredith, another well known novelist. Nelson spent his last night on English soil at Mickleham at the now "Burford Bridge Hotel", John Keats and Robert Louis Stevenson also stayed here.*

Another notable connection but not a human one, is Blair Athol, a horse. Blair Athol was stabled here in 1864 when he won the Derby. A fine 17th century pub, "The Running Horses" (free house), commemorates the event. The pub sign depicts the race on one side and the head of the winner on the other. Good beer can refresh the walker here but don't expect to win a race after it! The pub also serves good home made food. Mickleham church opposite the pub is Norman and well worth a visit. Note the wooden graves which are probably the best preserved of any in Surrey.

Just before the pub and opposite "Box Hill School", turn left along Dell Close to shortly pass a hall on your right and then Dell Close cottages on your left. At the end of the close pass through a small gate beside a larger iron gate and follow the path round to the left. The path is quite prominent and meanders through woodland in a northerly direction.

After approximately a quarter of a mile you meet a crossing track beside a flint wall, turn right to go up the hill on a bridleway marked by a white painted sign on a metal fence. The path becomes narrow and progresses diagonally uphill. At a "T" junction turn right on to a wide track recently created for wood and storm damage clearance, veering left after approximately 20 metres to continue uphill.

The path soon levels off and shortly meets a low wire fence on your left and continues through attractive woodland. At a fork veer left still following the fencing and on reaching a stile on your left, turn right. At a "T" junction turn right again and shortly after, turn left passing a wooden post and a National Trust sign for Box Hill to reach a large clearing with a trig point on your left, White Hill (142m).

Pass the trig point and shortly after veer left on to a wide grass track. This progresses into a wider track going north east along the top of White Hill. Follow the track as it goes very gently uphill to the crest where you should turn first right on to a prominent path leading downhill. Take care going downhill as this later becomes very steep and can be slippery and difficult to negotiate without good footwear.

At the bottom of the hill cross the road and join the public bridleway opposite passing a flint cottage, "Cockshott Cottage", on your right. This goes uphill between fields and then bends left through woodland to follow a perimeter wall on the right. Continue uphill following the wall until you come to a tarmac drive on to which you should turn left to pass High Ashurst Outdoor Centre on your right.

Stay on the drive passing a large house on your right "Bellasis" and soon after a small wood carving on your right of a miniature house on a tree stump with a keyhole as the entrance. Leave the drive as it bends left, taking the right fork, a gravel track passing houses on the left and soon after, prefabricated homes on your right. The track eventually arrives at a road, which you should cross to join the narrow public bridleway ahead. As a guide the total distance from Ashurst Outdoor Centre to the road is almost one and a quarter miles.

As the bridleway begins to descend ignore a turning on the left and continue straight on passing a giant chair carved from a tree stump on your right. You are now back on the North Downs Way marked by white acorn signs. Continue until you meet a path on your right marked by the acorn sign, and take this going steeply uphill up steps. At the top take the right hand fork still marked by the white acorn sign and continue on to meet a five bar gate marked "private". Turn left downhill and follow the path as it turns sharply right. This continues for some distance following white acorn signs all the way, to pass straight across a sunken crossing track by way of steps either side. N.B. For refreshments turn right on to the crossing track to "La Cellina", a freehouse and restaurant albeit not wholly suited to the walker. To continue our route, go straight on to go down and up another set of steps passing through woodland along the perimeter of the hill. You will eventually arrive at the wide open grass slopes of Box Hill with superb views of Dorking and the south. The path continues on, marked by the white acorns, until you reach a much wider path where you should turn right to arrive at the crest of Box Hill and the monument. Apart from excellent views, at weekends you will find hoards of people all seemingly fighting to be as close to each other as possible. Beware!

Box Hill 171m, (OS. 180512) *has been a popular recreation spot for years and has some diverse historical associations. Probably the earliest inhabitant still surviving today, is the Box tree from which the hill took its name. Jane Austen used the hill in her book Emma as the setting for a disastrous picnic and a local eccentric, Major Labelliere, used the hill as his final resting place, being buried upside down upon his own instruction. It is said his ghost now walks the hill and if you are ever on the hill when the wind and rain are at their strongest and the day trippers are safe at home in front of their television sets, then it is very easy to imagine this larger than life character wandering the hill side as he was famed for doing during stormy weather. A stone memorial now commemorates this unusual man.*

At the top of the hill "Swiss Cottage" (N.T.) was used by James Baird to experiment with television transmission. Today, Box Hill attracts people as it has for years for its unrivalled views across Surrey. Always the most crowded view point is the stone direction finder dedicated to Leopald Salomans of nearby "Norbury Park", who in 1914 gave Box Hill "to the nation".

Continue in front of the monument along the path around the hill where soon you will have excellent views over the Denbies vineyard from the early part of our walk. Shortly after, take the path on your left going directly downhill amongst box and yew trees. This path has been stepped to help walkers and protect the land from slippage in wet conditions.

At the bottom of the hill at a fork, veer left following the stone sign for the stepping stones.

N.B. If you do not wish to cross the river by the stepping stones, you can take the footbridge marked to the right as an alternative. Cross over the stepping stones and continue on to the parking area and the main road, the A24, the start of our walk. Incidentally, if you are driving back through Dorking, look out for the town boundary signs headed by a cockrell. Dorking used to be Surrey's centre for poultry and is home to a breed of hen which is unique, having five claws instead of the normal four.

ACCOMMODATION

The Burford Bridge Hotel (THF), West Humble. Tel: 0306 884561

Half a mile from the walk. On the banks of the river Mole at the foot of Box Hill, the Burford Bridge Hotel is set in a natural beauty spot complimented by the hotel's well cared for grounds. The hotel is full of history, Nelson spent his last night here before the Battle of Trafalgar. The hotel has good restaurants and an outdoor heated swimming pool.

The Running Horses, Mickleham. Tel: 0372 372590

On the walk, the Running Horses is a very local pub serving good bar food and beer. It also has an excellent restaurant and offers bed and breakfast accommodation. The pub is in a good location opposite the village church. An excellent choice at the end of a hard day's walking.

Youth Hostel, Tanners Hatch YHA, Polesden Lacey, Dorking. Tel: 0372 52528

Half a mile from the walk, Tanners Hatch is an isolated cottage (you can only reach it by foot). Situated in the woods of Ranmore common the hostel has no electricity so bring your own lighting. Camping is also permitted.

Camping, Polesden Lacey, Dorking. Tel: 0372 456844

On the walk, this is a Camping and Caravanning Club site in a beautiful setting on an old cricket pitch in the grounds of Polesden Lacey House, N.T. Please note, only tents and trailers are permitted.

THE GUNPOWDER ENCOUNTER

Distance: $11^3/_4$ miles (19 km)

Time: Allow approximately 5 hours, more if possible to explore the villages.

Map: Ordnance Survey Landranger Maps 186 and 187

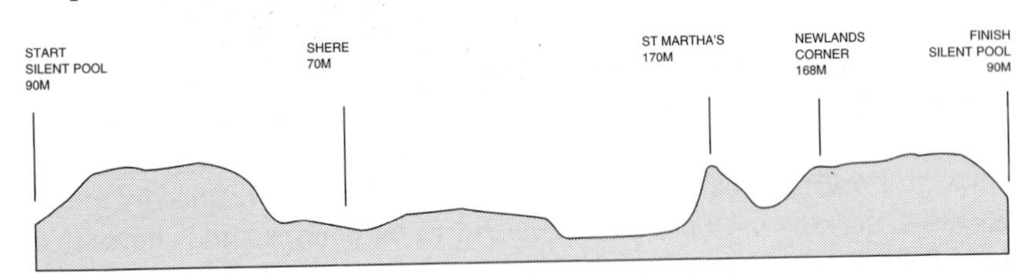

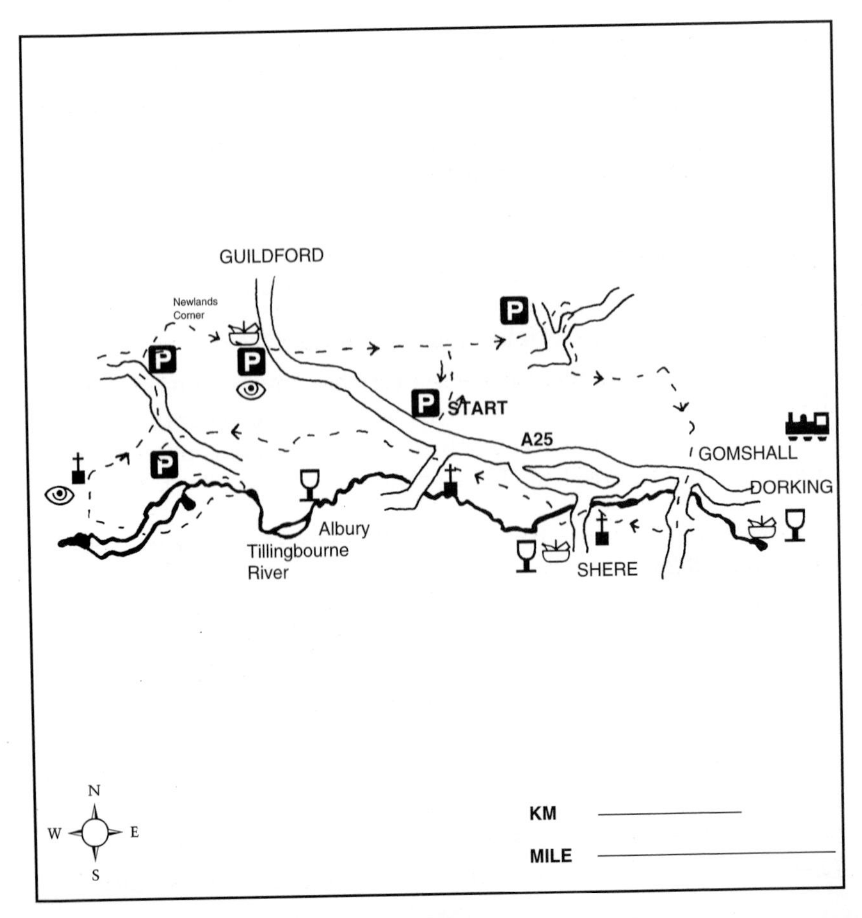

Walk Summary

The Gunpowder Encounter takes you through some of the best known beauty spots in Surrey. You are constantly rewarded with stunning views, picture postcard properties and all around an ever changing landscape which pleasantly surprises. The walk also in parts follows the beautiful Tillingbourne river, passing several mill ponds and the remains of the gunpowder industry, hence the walk's title.

The mill ponds are home for a wonderful variety of ducks as well as swans so if you have any stale bread bring it with you. The walk is fairly easy going except for two steep climbs and one steep descent which can be slippery in wet weather. Parts of the walk can also be muddy.

Start - OS. 060485 Map 187

The walk starts from the Silent Pool car park situated on the northern side of the A25 between Guildford and Shere, almost opposite the turn off for the A248. Other possible starting points are the car park at Newlands Corner (OS. 044493 Map 186) also situated on the A25 two miles west of the Silent Pool car park, or Gomshall village (OS. 085478 Map 187) which has a railway station. If you start from Newlands Corner or Gomshall a detour will be required if you wish to visit the Silent Pool.

THE GUNPOWDER ENCOUNTER

Follow the path past Sherebourne farm and then through the gate leading to the Silent Pool (Sherebourne Farm has a Farm Animal Centre open to the public). Continue along side a pool to a second pool, the Silent Pool.

The Silent Pool (OS. 061486 Map 187), *occupies an ancient quarry fed by a natural spring and has been a valuable source of pure water sometimes even guarded over the centuries. Its haunting beauty though, has a more sinister side. According to local legend, the daughter of a woodman once drowned here whilst bathing. The story goes that whilst she was bathing a nobleman rode up and seeing her naked started making advances. The frightened girl fought him off and in a rage, the nobleman mounted his horse and drove her deeper into the pool where, unable to swim, the girl drowned. It was her father who found her body and floating with it the hat belonging to the nobleman. It is said that the hat bore the emblem of the monarch, King John himself. The girl is supposed to haunt the pool and is said to be responsible for the unique stillness for which the pool is noted.*

Whether you believe the tale or not the pool does have a presence and it is worth stopping for a few minutes to experience its beauty.

Continue straight ahead and up the steps at the far end of the pool, turning immediately left thereafter and then right at the edge of a field. Going uphill, the path leaves the field on your left and enters woodland passing an old pill box on your right. As you climb the hill take time to stop and admire the view behind you, especially to the west over Guildford. Ignore all tracks to the left and right of the path and continue on for a quarter of a mile, though it may seem longer, to reach the beginnings of a wood and a prominent crossroads.

Turn right at this point joining the signposted public bridleway - you are now on the North Downs Way. Continue along the North Downs Way, until you reach a car park, passing on your way Surrey Open Space signs on the left and, where clearings allow, good views to your right. Ignore all crossing tracks. Go through the car park passing a picnic area, cross over the small road and continue straight along the path. Carry on until you reach another road just before which you will see a small man-made pond on your left. Turn right along the road and then almost immediately left on to a track signposted North Downs Way.

Follow the white acorn signs and ignore two large tracks which join the track you are on from the right, one shortly after the other, and bear left at some houses where it is signposted to continue on the North Downs Way. Pass some houses and stables on your left. This is "Hollister Farm". The farm occupies a site on which it is believed there once stood a brothel, frequently visited by the infamous monarch King John.

Pass through a small wooden gateway ahead and continue on through woodland. After some distance cross over a track, on the right of which there is a concrete water tank and continue on for half a mile, ignoring all joining tracks which are in the main fenced preventing access, until you reach another, smaller marked crossing.

At this point turn right to join a bridleway. This eventually narrows into a small path between trees and gradually descends passing a pillbox on your right, just above which are good views to the south west. Immediately thereafter, you will arrive at a small clearing and marked footpath (yellow arrow) on your right, this time with good views of Gomshall. Take the footpath on your right, at first almost turning back on yourself, and after approximately 10 paces turn left downhill.

You will very quickly join another path where you should turn left and continue downhill passing through an area full of Buddleia bushes, which in summer is a mass of butterflies. You will soon see parkland on your right, belonging to "Netley House", a private estate.

Netley House (OS. 078484 Map 187)*, derives its name from the Abbey of Netley in Hampshire which owned the land in the 13th century. The original Netley House was on the site of the present Netley Farm on the other side of the A25 and in all probability, was a farm house for the Cistercian white monks of Netley Abbey. The house which you can see today was built circa. 1790 by Edmund Shallett Lomax. It was enlarged in 1860 by his daughter, Mrs. John Fraser, following a fire which all but destroyed the interior of the house.*

On your left you will pass a number of small houses to continue on down through an avenue of yew trees to the main road, the A25. For refreshments, turn left at the main road to visit Gomshall.

Gomshall (OS. 085478 Map 187)*, is famous for its tanneries and one still exists even to this day. In fact it is claimed to be the oldest tannery in the country, dating back to the 11th century. The tannery now has a shop from which it sells the goods produced.*

"The King John House", which the walk passes is Jacobean and used to be called "The Old Tannery House". In its garden there was once another tannery. At its height, Gomshall had three tanneries.

One other traditional trade which exists in Gomshall is the making of archery targets. This successful business was started in 1950 by Maurice Egerton after closing the Gomshall mill. Our walk will shortly pass its current site.

If you require refreshments you can visit "The Compasses" (Gibbs Mews), a large attractive pub in the centre of the village. The pub has a separate bar serving food. There is also a Post Office and garage, both selling light refreshments.

To continue our route, cross the main road and follow the small road, Queen Street, almost immediately opposite, passing "The King John House" on your right. Continue along Queen Street, which initially runs adjacent to the Tillingbourne river, and on between houses ignoring the first road on your right (New Road), to take the next small lane on your right called Gravelpits Lane opposite "Gomshall Lodge".

Just before "Gravelpits Cottages", take the track on your left to reach a junction of tracks, at which you should fork right between two houses, "Highlands" and "Gravelpits Farmhouse".

Continue on passing between fields with a good view now on your right of "Netley House". The path gradually descends and passes through a small gate into a field, and as you continue to the brow of the hill you will see on your right the church spire and village of Shere and above this, "Shere Manor".

Just before a large farm gate, pass through a small wooden gate immediately to the right, following the path which leads down to Shere church, St. James'.

Shere village and St. James' church (OS. 074478 Map 187). *This picture postcard village attracts visitors from all over the world. The church which is the jewel in a very impressive crown, is well worth a visit. A church has stood on this site for over 1000 years, though the present church dates from 1190AD. Its excellent stained glass windows contain some of the oldest glass in the country. One of the main attractions are the brasses, among the best being a memorial to Robert Scarcliff, a former rector and Lord Audley. An unusual feature is the 14th century quatre foil and squint in the north wall of the chancel. These were apertures to a cell in which "The Anchoress of Shere", Christine daughter of William the carpenter, was walled up in the service of God. Through the apertures, Christine made her contact with the church.*

Another notable feature is the Crusader Alms Coffer. This large oak chest, which dates from about 1200AD was used to collect and house gifts to support the crusades. As you leave the church look for bricks inscribed with initials in the church yard wall. These belong to villagers who were responsible for the upkeep of the wall.

The name Shere is derived from the Saxon name Essira and at the time of the Doomsday Book, thirty families held residence here. After the Norman conquest, Shere passed into the ownership of William de Warren, Earl of Surrey. For several hundred years it continuously changed hands, eventually passing to Lord Audley. Following his son's involvement in a rebellion against Henry VII, he was beheaded in 1497AD and Henry VII gave the manor to Sir Reginald Bray. The Bray family apart from an early interruption, continued to hold the manor over the centuries and still live in the village today.

One well known resident of Shere was Sir Alfred Gilbert, the sculpture of Eros at Piccadilly Circus. He lived at Shere in the 1890's. For refreshments, the village has several shops and two good pubs, "The Prince of Wales" (Youngs) a friendly local pub, and the 17th century "White Horse" (Chef & Brewer), which offers an extensive menu.

From the church follow the road, with houses on your left, into the village to the "White Horse" pub. Cross the road in front the of pub, turn right and then immediately left into Lower Street, where you will once more follow the Tillingbourne river. Towards the end of Lower Street, with particularly pretty cottages (look out for "The Old Prison" on your left), turn right and cross over a small ford by way of the footbridge. Continue uphill until you reach the first property on your left, "The Old Rectory", to the right of which is a small somewhat concealed, but marked, footpath.

Take this footpath running parallel with the wall of "The Old Rectory", crossing over a small lane and continuing on the path ahead. Shortly after, you should pass through a kissing gate to cross a field, passing the Albury estate on your left.

i ***Albury Park (OS. 063477 Map 187)*** *is the original site of the village of Albury. However, the Lord of the manor preferring to live alone, persuaded the villagers, no doubt with some help, to move to the village's present site. Today only a Saxon church remains from the original village. Henry Drummond bought the estate in 1819 and set about modernising the Tudor manor house. The architect he employed was Pugin, better known for the magnificent stone work on the Houses of Parliament. Pugin had a fascination for chimneys, and when he had finished the manor it had, and still has, sixty three chimneys, every single one different. An excellent example of his work can be seen in Albury village itself, where many of the houses appear to be built as nothing more than elaborate stands for the tall ornate chimneys they support. The landscaping of Albury Park is credited to Evelyn of Wotton.*

At the other side of the field go through another gate and up the small track between trees and follow this crossing over a large double track, which again is part of the Albury estate. Cross over a stile into a field and walk towards the large church ahead.

i ***The Catholic Apostolic church (OS. 061482 Map 187)*** *was founded by Henry Drummond in the mid-nineteenth century, the then owner of the Albury estate. Its building came about following riots in 1830 in protest of the famine in the area. Looking for a saviour the poor turned to God and religious fever spread with the word that the second advent of Christ was near. Henry Drummond got caught up in the new preachings and built the church to their cause. Unfortunately, the church always seems to be locked, though this may change in the future.*

At the other side of the field, cross the stile and go down the track passing a small cottage and the church on your left until you reach a road, the A248. If your legs are on strike you can at the road turn right along the pavement, to cross over the main road, A25, ahead and return to the car park at the Silent Pool from where our walk commenced.

To continue the walk, cross the A248 and the stile opposite and follow the footpath along the right hand perimeter of a field. Go over a stile and continue straight on to another stile which you should cross to walk along the edge of Weston Wood. Cross a concrete track leading to a sandpit works, and continue straight on along a marked fenced path, passing out buildings on your right.

When the path meets a junction continue straight ahead on to a wider track, leading to "Timber Croft" cottage. Pass in front of the cottage, do not turn right. The track, which is part of the original Pilgrims Way, begins to descend with Weston Wood still on your left and open views to your right, ultimately leaving the wood to pass between open fields.

On reaching a "T" junction after some cottages, turn left and then almost immediately right on to a path marked public bridleway, leading up the side of a steep slope. The path soon levels out and continues with woodland on your left and views to the North Downs on the right. Pass through a small wooden gate on to a fenced path between fields. Ahead to your right is "Newbarn Farm". When the path reaches another "T" junction, turn right heading towards the farm and follow the path as it bends round to the left (do not go straight on), i.e. staying on the public bridleway and not the footpath. This leads gently uphill at the top of which there are good views behind you of the North Downs. Shortly after, the bridleway leaves the wooded area to continue between fenced fields to reach a lane. Cross the lane on to a sandy track which veers left and leads into a car park signposted "St. Martha's".

Turn right into the car park and take the left hand fork which is a narrow grass path as opposed to the alternative sandy track. After about 20 paces you reach another fork at which you should bear left, to do the same at the next two forks, i.e. bearing left all the time, to proceed steeply downhill through woodland, (the path can be very steep and slippery in wet weather). This veers left upon meeting a field and leads down through more woodland.

You will shortly see the Tillingbourne river on the right and the path will follow high above this until you meet a white house on your right, "Millstream Cottage". Turn right in front of the house and continue on. The attractive pond on your left is Waterloo Pond and is an old mill pond. The confusing course of the Tillingbourne through the valley is the result of the numerous mills in the area which diverted the river's course to their chosen sites. Consequently, at times, the Tillingbourne has the appearance of being several rivers.

If you need a pitstop before continuing, recharge your batteries by turning left at the house and follow the path skirting the pond to reach

Albury village and the "Drummond Arms Inn", a free house. The diversion is one and a half miles each way so be absolutely sure you need that drink!

To continue our route, walk along the drive way which bends round to the right to follow another arm of the Tillingbourne, to reach "Albury Mill Trout Farm" with an attractive mill pond on your left.

Albury Mill (OS. 039480 Map 186). *Records show that there has been a mill near this spot since 1255AD. This mill survived in one form or another until 1830, when the mill was burnt to the ground. The fire was started deliberately by James Warner, who shot at the owner of the mill, James Frank, as he tried to stop him. James Frank was unable to stop the mill burning to the ground, but he did help in apprehending the arsonist and James Warner became the last man in England to hang for arson. The mill you see today was built at the turn of the century by one Charles Bolting.*

In addition to the trout farm there is also a country shop. Walk in front of the mill and shop along the drive way until you reach a public footpath sign ahead of you to the right. Follow this footpath along the perimeter of a house, over a stile and into a field and continue across the field along a well trodden path. To your right below Colyers Hanger (Hanger is an old name for a steep tree covered slope) is a beautiful lake surrounded by reed beds. This is a haven for wildlife and is frequented by numerous species of wildfowl.

Cross another stile and follow the path, running adjacent to a ditch, diagonally right across the field. The ruined buildings visible on your right are the remains of old gunpowder mills.

The Gunpowder Mills (along Tillingbourne valley - Map 186). *Watching the Tillingbourne bubble and tumble between tranquil mill ponds and wooded slopes, it is hard to believe that this innocent delight of the Surrey countryside was ever associated with gunpowder. However, right up until the early part of this century, gunpowder was manufactured along the river banks in this valley, evidence of which can still be seen today. The first gunpowder manufacture started in 1580 and other mills soon spread. The success of the industry brought its share of misery and several accidents resulted in many fatalities, including an incident in 1901 when six men were killed in an explosion. Today, the many derelict buildings of the gunpowder industry lie in silence along the banks of the Tillingbourne, their presence a memorial to the unfortunate people who died from their trade.*

Go over the next stile and cross the field to reach and cross another stile into a lane where you should turn right over a bridge. If you wish to take a closer look at some remains of the old gunpowder mills, turn left immediately after the bridge, the ruins of an old factory and mill are only 100m distance beside another diverted arm of the Tillingbourne. Our walk however, continues along the lane over another bridge, after which you should take the left hand fork uphill. Ignore a turning to your right signposted The Downs Link and continue straight ahead between hedged banks. After some distance, take the next public footpath on your right approximately 40 paces before a tarmac drive. Go uphill passing "Chilworth Manor" on your left.

i ***Chilworth Manor (OS. 026478 Map 186),*** *dates originally from Saxon times though the present building is 17th century. The manor has some fine terraces created with the building of the house. The walled garden, which can be seen from the path, was added in the 18th century by the Duchess of Marlborough. In the summer the house and garden are regularly open to the public. If you are lucky enough to pass on such an occasion, you could do a lot worse than to stop and have a privileged look around.*

Continue up the steep path which seems to last forever, stopping to catch your breath and the view. You can now understand why John Bunyan called this the "hill of difficulty" in his book, Pilgrims Progress. As you near the top of the hill cross a wide crossing track and continue ahead to pass a fenced waterworks on your left. Suddenly St. Martha's church comes into view ahead of you.

i ***The church of St. Martha 170m/573 feet (OS. 028484 Map 186).*** *This remarkable hill has been the sight of a church for over 1000 years and before that, there is evidence of bronze age activity on the southern slopes. The traditional explanation of the church's dedication is that Martha is a derivation of martyr. Martyr because the hill is associated with the slaying of early Christians by pagan Saxons. The church indeed dates from Saxon times, though there is no visible evidence of this early construction left. The tower was built in 1850 by the architect Henry Woodyear, the original tower having collapsed in 1763 as a result of a gunpowder explosion.*

The Pilgrims Way passed the bottom of the hill and the church became an important stop for those travelling to Canterbury. There is evidence in the church that many of these pilgrims travelled from overseas and the parish of St. Martha uses the scallop shell, a badge from Compostella in

Spain, another place of pilgrimage as its emblem. One final point of interest, on a clear day the excellent view from the hill can take in parts of eight counties.

ST. MARTHA'S CHURCH

Turn right in front of the church to follow a wide sandy track downhill. On nearing the bottom of the hill, you reach a fork where you should take the left hand path, marked with a blue arrow and white acorn. As you join this, ignore the path which turns immediately left and continue ahead, descending gently following the white acorns to reach a lane beside a cottage on your left. Do not join the lane, but take a path parallel to the lane still following the sign for the North Downs Way. This can be extremely muddy in wet weather and requires good footwear.

The path climbs slowly uphill and ends when you reach some steps which you should go down to cross the lane and follow the footpath the other side. Almost immediately after joining this path, turn left at the white acorn sign, on to a narrower path which can be easily missed, and follow this round to the right. On reaching the open hill side, turn left and follow the perimeter of the hill to White Lane car park.

Go across the car park to join a footpath marked by a wooden post with a butterfly, next to the White Lane information sign. Pass between yew trees and follow the path to reach a wide track which you cross to follow another narrow path straight ahead. This meanders through a mixture of woodland and open bracken known locally as The Roughs, and is marked in places by posts with a deer.

Ignore all joining paths and continue on to a crossroads. Go straight across the wide crossing track and continue along the path again ignoring all joining and crossing paths until you arrive at the large car park at Newlands Corner.

Newlands Corner 168m/567 feet (OS. 44493 Map 186), *has been a popular view point for years. Today, its popularity means a hamburger bar, public toilets and large car park, which on a weekend is packed with people admiring the view from their cars, windows down to take in* *the fresh country air! If you can ignore all this, the view from here is magnificent and the burgers are good too. The long sweep of the yew trees along the top of the hill have been a landmark for centuries and are even mentioned in the Domesday Book.*

Turn left and continue through the car park to the other side to meet a small path on your right just before the main road, marked by a post with a butterfly. Go straight over a crossing track following the sign in the direction of the North Downs Way. Cross the main road, A25, pass through a wooden gate beside a Surrey County Council Open Space sign and continue straight on through woodland.

Pass a view point with seating on your right and continue straight along the top of the hill, ignoring a marked path joining from your right. After approximately one mile you will reach a crossroads. Turn right and retrace your steps going downhill past the Silent Pool to the car park.

ACCOMMODATION

The Manor Hotel, Newlands Corner, Guildford. Tel: 0483 222624

Half a mile from the walk, situated in nine acres of parkland. This rather grand hotel started as a Victorian country house. All the rooms are extremely comfortable and the hotel has the advantage of being close to Newlands Corner, an alternative starting point to the walk. It even has a helicopter pad, useful in emergencies, if you have overdone the walking or the local brew!

Crossways Farm, Abinger Hammer, Dorking. Tel: 0306 730173

One and three quarter miles from the walk, Crossways Farm is a Jacobean farmhouse built in the early part of the 17th century. Its entrance is through a lovely walled garden up a stone flagged path. Inside a great oak staircase leads up to comfortable rooms. If you wish to continue the magic of the olde worlde villages you have explored on your walk, then Crossways is a must.

Youth Hostel, Tanners Hatch YHA, Polesden Lacey, Dorking. Tel: 0372 52528

Eleven miles from the walk, Tanners Hatch, is an isolated cottage (you can only reach it by foot). Situated in the woods of Ranmore Common, the hostel has no electricity, so bring your own lighting. Camping is also permitted.

Camping, Polesden Lacey, Dorking. Tel: 0372 456844

Twelve miles from the walk, this is a Camping and Caravanning Club site in a beautiful setting on an old cricket pitch in the grounds of Polesden Lacey House, N.T. Please note, that only tents and trailer tents are permitted.

ALL ABOUT EVELYN

Distance: $12\frac{1}{2}$ miles (20 km)

Time: Allow approximately 5 hours

Map: Ordnance Survey Landranger Map 187

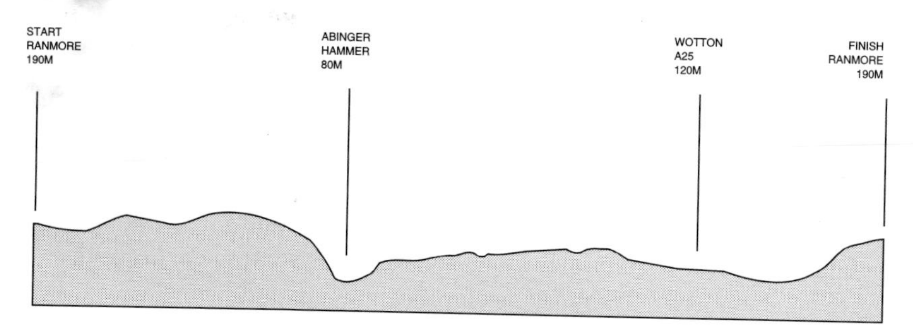

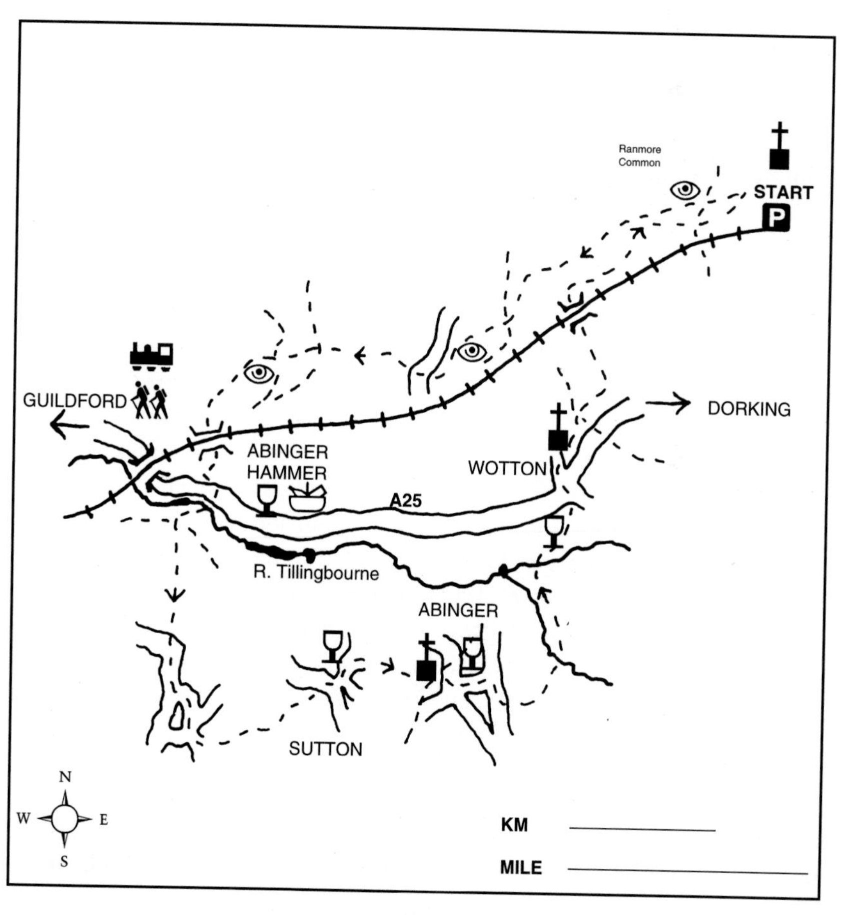

Walk Summary

All About Evelyn explores the countryside surrounding the great Wotton estate, once home to the famous diarist John Evelyn. As you walk you will quickly begin to understand why Evelyn so appreciated where he lived and wrote so fondly of it in his diaries. Part of the route follows the North Downs Way with good views to the south and the countryside through which you later tread.

The lowland part of the walk takes you past historic Wotton House and through some of the more remote hamlets in Surrey, unchanged through the ravages of time. There is a lot to see so allow plenty of time and you will find the walk all the more enjoyable. The going can be very muddy in winter particularly along the North Downs, so ensure you have good footwear. There is one significant ascent and one descent, otherwise the walk is reasonably level.

Start - OS. 143504 Map 187

The walk starts from the car park on the edge of Ranmore Common, off of Ranmore Common road close to the Ranmore church, St. Barnabas. If coming from London or the M25, take the A24 south towards Dorking and just before reaching Dorking, take the turning right signposted to Guildford. On meeting a mini roundabout go straight across and at a "T" junction turn right. The car park is at the top of the hill on the left, shortly after two cottages on the same side.

If coming from the east or south, from the roundabout at Dorking where the A24 and A25 cross, take the A24 north towards Leatherhead. Turn left at the first set of traffic lights to reach the mini roundabout mentioned above. Coming from the west, take the A25 and just as you reach Dorking, turn left following the signs to Leatherhead and Ranmore. Look out for another turning on your left, Station road, signposted to West Station, Ranmore and Effingham Business Park. Follow this road to the top of the hill where you will find the car park on your left. Dorking has two railway stations close to the start, Dorking and Dorking West. There is also a station at Gomshall which is close to Abinger Hammer from where you can join the walk.

ALL ABOUT EVELYN

P From the car park go over the stile next to the information board and take the first path going diagonally right, heading towards trees and passing a red brick house on your right. As you proceed you will have good views left of Leith Hill and the Greensand Ridge and behind you of Dorking. The path you are on follows the top of the hill heading for a gate and stile. Go over the stile and join the path ahead marked by a white acorn, indicating that you are now on the North Downs Way. Stay on the main path following the top of the hill, marked by white acorn signs, ignoring all joining paths. After approximately half a mile you will pass an old gate with a stile on your left and shortly after meet a wooden fence ahead marked with a yellow arrow. Pass through a gap in the fencing and go over a crossing track to continue on the path ahead and after approximately a quarter of a mile go straight over another crossing track, still following the North Downs Way. Beech trees have been in evidence since we started but now they take over bringing an elegance to the woodland which makes this part of the walk particularly attractive. Narrowing, the path beings to veer right uphill to skirt a large hollow, Pickets Hole.

You will eventually meet a prominent path coming in from the right. Turn left on to the path which descends to reach a small gate beside a pill box. Pass through the gate and turn almost immediately right, leaving the main path, to go up a small slope and over a stile to continue along the top of the hill, still following the white acorn signs. The path passes another pill box and shortly after reaches a stile with a yellow arrow. Go over the stile to follow the path ahead which brings you out on to more open hillside. Going across the hillside you will pass yet another pill box to reach a narrow lane.

i ***Pill Boxes, White and Hackhurst Downs.*** *The North Downs were an important line of defence for London during the Second World War. The numerous pill boxes you pass were part of the defence and were manned by the Canadian army which had an army base on Hackhurst Downs. It is said that the pill boxes were so well constructed that it was too expensive for them to be demolished. Today they remain as an interesting but sombre reminder of those unsettled times.*

Turn right along the lane and after approximately 25 paces, turn left on to a footpath signposted as the North Downs Way. This shortly bends left following the white acorn signs and then proceeds along the top of the hill. You will soon arrive at a gate through which you should pass, a National Trust sign informs you that you are now on White Down Lease.

The wide path you are on leads across White Down Lease with superb views to your left of Leith and Holmbury Hill. You must now stay on the path for half a mile, ignoring all turnings off, to reach Blatchford Down announced by a National Trust sign. Go over a stile to cross a large track and go over another stile to follow a path ahead which eventually leads to a wooden gate. If in doubt remember to follow the white acorn signs. Pass through the gate and go straight over a crossing path the other side, continuing through woodland to eventually arrive at a large track which is evidently popular with four wheel drive vehicles. Turn left down the track following a red arrow and after a short distance pass a white acorn sign on your right, thereby leaving the North Downs Way.

The track goes steeply downhill and can at times be extremely muddy so great care is needed. At the bottom of the hill the track crosses fields to pass under a railway arch and continues to reach a main road, the A25. In front of you at this point is "Frog Island" vegetarian restaurant and a trout farm. Cross the road and turn left along the pavement, passing an antique and junk shop and on your left, "Hunters Moon Farm", an intriguing name for a farm I've always thought. Shortly after the farm, take the first public bridleway right on to a wide track. If you wish to visit Abinger Hammer however, continue along the pavement and the famous clock overhanging the A25 will soon come into view.

Abinger Hammer (OS. 095475 Map 187) *dissected by the A25 and the more attractive Tillingbourne river, is famous for its picturesque village clock. The clock erected in memory of Lord Farrer of "Abinger Hall", hangs precariously over the A25 with an iron worker striking the hour. It acts as an indicator to the importance of the iron industry, once prevalent in this area. Today the hammer ponds have been taken over by watercress beds. In summer cricket is played on the cricket green beside the Tillingbourne and this can be a pleasant place to rest.*

For refreshments, there is a s-mall shop, a tea room which also serves good food and "The Abinger Arms" pub (Friary Meux). "The Abinger Arms" used to be a tannery before it started serving fine ales, the pub food also comes recommended. Despite the busy A25, Abinger Hammer remains a village worth exploring.

Follow the track passing some houses on your right to cross the Tillingbourne and shortly after, take the first turning left on to a marked bridleway. Do not make the mistake of staying on the concrete track or taking the second bridleway which starts between the track and the bridleway you are about to take.

Follow the first bridleway uphill between banks ignoring a stile on your right and all joining paths to eventually meet a crossing path. Cross this to continue straight ahead now passing between houses and gardens. This then leads out on to a drive way on which you should continue to meet a tarmac lane where you should turn right. Follow the lane to meet a road which you should cross and turn left along the pavement, passing a telephone and post box. Follow the pavement until you meet Hoe Lane on your left into which you should turn.

The lane bends round to the right and shortly after at a farm gate on your right, there are good views across the fields to "Lane End Farm". Ignore the road on your left which is in fact the continuation of Hoe Lane, to continue straight ahead passing pretty cottages on your right. As the lane bends right leave this to join a lane ahead signposted as Franks Field. Follow this for a short distance and turn left along a track immediately after "Keepers Cottage", signposted "Private Drive to Timbers Ridge, Footpath Only". Pass to the right of "Timbers Ridge Cottage" and join a narrow path leading to a stile ahead.

Cross the stile into a large field and go across the centre of the field along a well trodden path. Cross a stile at the other side of the field and continue straight downhill along a narrow path, ignoring the path on your right. This descends into a narrow picturesque valley and then climbs uphill towards some houses. Go over a stile and continue along a path between houses to shortly join a drive way. After approximately 30 metres when the drive way bends round to the left, leave it to continue ahead along a narrow footpath between gardens.

On reaching a narrow lane turn left passing an information board on your right with a map of the hamlet, Sutton Place. Ignore a lane on your left opposite the sign and follow the lane you are on as it descends gently. Near the bottom as the lane bends left look out for an unmarked footpath on your right by an old farm gate. Take this footpath which now follows the left hand perimeter of a field uphill and continue to the far left hand corner of the field to pass through a metal barrier on to a lane.

Turn left along the lane and after 20 paces turn right opposite "Stile Cottage", on to a narrow fenced footpath running between fields. Half way across, the path descends with beautiful views over the hamlet of Sutton Abinger and "The Volunteer" pub. Soon after, the path leads down some steps to a road. Turn right along the road and then first left into Raikes Lane. To your right there are some beautiful half timber cottages which make up the hamlet of Sutton Abinger. "The Volunteer" pub (Friary Meux) ahead, is equally attractive and has a beautiful location overlooking a stream which runs into the Tillingbourne. The pub garden is of neat terraces cut into the hillside with views across the valley to Sutton. The pub also serves food which makes it a pleasant stop.

Our route continues along the lane passing the pub and ignoring a road on your right. Follow the lane climbing gently uphill between steep banks known as Raikes Hollow and after approximately 200 metres leave it by way of some steep steps on your right. There is a handrail for assistance. At the top of the steps go over a stile into a field and turn left to follow the perimeter to another stile beside a large farm gate. Cross the stile and turn right along a farm track which shortly runs between open fields with excellent views to your left of the North Downs and the early part of our walk. Pass over a cattle grid and continue along a wide grass track between fields heading for Abinger Common, the buildings of which are visible ahead. Cross a stile and follow a narrower track ahead passing "Abinger Manor" on your right, the site of an old Norman castle where the remains of a moat are still visible. The path bends round to lead into the church yard of St. James through which you should pass to reach a road and "The Abinger Hatch" pub ahead, a free house serving good food.

Abinger Common (OS. 115460 Map 187) *was once claimed to be the oldest village in England following the discovery of a Mesolithic pit dwelling found within its boundaries. Today, the village still detaches itself from the modern world. The Norman church, despite being hit by a flying bomb in 1944, retains its charm. On the green a set of stocks still remain, reputedly never used. The church is dedicated to St. James who is the patron saint of pilgrims, the church being close to the Pilgrims Way. The 17th century "Abinger Manor" was built by John Evelyn. It stands on the site of a former Norman stronghold. The motte, which can be seen from the path, was surrounded by a moat fed by a natural spring. Part of the moat still remains, the spring continuing to do its duty to this day.*

THE ABINGER HATCH PUB

Turn right in front of the pub and follow the road passing a duck pond with resident ducks and take the first lane left shortly after. Take note of the sign somewhat hidden in the holly referring to "Locomotives"and "Heavy Motor Cars". The lane goes downhill to pass "The Old Rectory" and then climbs uphill to meet a "T" junction where you should turn right. Shortly after passing through some old wooden posts either side of the road, turn left on to a signposted public bridleway. Stay on the bridleway, ignoring all joining paths and at a fork take the left fork and follow this all the way to meet a lane beside an entrance to the Wotton estate.

Turn left along the lane for approximately 10 paces and then left on to a drive way signposted as a public footpath, to pass through a large white gate marked "Pugs Corner". Follow the drive way downhill passing woodland and thereafter a lovely property on your left. As the drive way bends left towards the property leave this and turn right on to a signposted public footpath, which runs between fenced fields to meet a stile. Cross over the stile and go over a pretty stone bridge which acts as a dam to a stream and turn left to cross another stile beside a large wooden gate. Continue along a wide footpath which follows a shallow valley with the stream descending by way of a series of miniature weirs. Ignore a wide path on your right and continue on looking out for a large property on your left, "Wotton House".

Wotton House (OS. 122469 Map 187) *was for years the seat of the great Evelyn family, arguably the most important family Surrey has ever had. Though no longer living in the house certain members of the family still live on the estate. The Evelyns will always be famous for introducing gunpowder into Britain, an industry which blossomed in the Tillingbourne valley nearby (see Gunpowder Encounter). However, the most famous member of the Evelyn family will always be John Evelyn, the diarist.*

Born in 1620, John Evelyn grew up in Wotton House taking a great interest in all that surrounded him. He was a great naturalist and rare for those days, a conservationist. It is he we must thank for the extensive woodland around Leith Hill. He became famous for his garden designs and introduced many new trees to the south of England, including the now popular firs. His close friend, Henry Capel, went on to found Kew Gardens. John Evelyn's most notable achievement however, was his diaries. Every day was recorded in fine detail, the entries not only gave account of his own activities but of national and international happenings along with his opinions. The result is a valuable insight into life in the late 17th century. The diaries which are now housed at Christchurch College, Oxford, are recognised as being one of the most important contributions to the history of Surrey.

For a man who took such great care over his environment, it was a cruel twist of fate that three years before his death, storms similar to that of 1987, struck Surrey flattening much of his beloved Wotten estate. The following day, November 27th, 1703, Evelyn looked out to survey the damage and in his diary he wrote "the late dreadful hurricane subverted so many thousands of good oaks, prostrating the trees, laying them in ghastly postures like whole regiments of soldiers fallen in battle by the sword of the conqueror".

The house which you can see through the trees today was built in the early 19th century, the house that John Evelyn knew being the victim of another disaster, a fire in 1800. It is associated with many ghosts, one of the more well known being that of Bishop Wilberforce who was thrown from his horse on his way to see Evelyn. A monument to this unfortunate event can be found on the North Downs near Abinger Hammer.

The path then bends round to the right and meets a crossing track, where you should turn right and then immediately left on to a narrow path going downhill. Go over a stile and cross the Tillingbourne, at this point a stream, and go across the field ahead to a stile. Go over the stile on to the drive way to "Wotton House" and turn right along the drive leading away from the house.

Soon after the drive way bends round to the left, you will reach a stile on your right which you should cross into a field. Go diagonally left over the field heading for a large metal gate and stile, to the right of a small wooden clubhouse. Cross over the stile into a car park and continue ahead to pass "The Wotton Hatch", a Fullers pub serving a wide selection of food.

Cross the main road, the A25, in front of the pub and follow the lane ahead leading to the church of St. John the Evangelist. Some time before the church, turn right over the first stile beside a metal farm gate and follow the right hand perimeter of the field down into the valley. If you wish to visit the church continue straight on. You can rejoin the route by crossing the field to the right (east) of the church proceeding diagonally right down into the valley.

i

Wotton Church (OS. 126480 Map 187). *This unusual 13th century church has one of the best settings of any church in Surrey. Standing on high ground surrounded by fields with the North Downs as a backdrop, the church makes a fitting resting place for John Evelyn. It was in this church Evelyn recalls, that he started his first lessons. They were conducted by a friar and were always held in the porch. Evelyn, along with three generations of his family, are buried at the church. A* *mausoleum to the north of the church lists the total eighteen Evelyn family members buried here.*

John Evelyn made it quite clear however, that he had no wish to be buried in the mausoleum and his tomb, along with that of his wife Mary, lie in the floor of the chapel. Before you leave the church, look for a set of eight heads carved above the south door. They are in fairly poor condition now but it is said that they once represented a priest, a baron, a king, a queen, a peasant, an archbishop (Stephan Langton), a pupal legate and a pope. If the interpretation is right, it is the earliest known carving in England of a pope.

Our route continues through the field and passes a pond on your right, shortly after which it bends left to pass a stile on the right which you should ignore. The path leads down between banks to a stile beside a farm gate in front of some houses. Go over the stile and continue straight on passing a post box on your left. Ignore a narrow marked footpath beside the last property on your left and continue along a wide track going east. Ignore a track joining from the left and continue straight on to shortly after turn left on to another track heading towards "Stockmans Coomb Farm" and the North Downs.

Pass "Coomb Farm" on your right and soon after follow the track round to the right passing the farm buildings of "Stockmans Coomb Farm". On your left is a stone carving studio which is open to visitors.

The track, which can be very muddy, bends round to the left and winds between fields to pass under a railway line. Ahead to your right at this point on the top of the hill, you can see the church spire of St. Barnabas which is near the end of our walk. Continue on to reach the tree line and pass through a small wooden gate turning right to follow a marked bridleway along the bottom of the North Downs.

Some time after pass through another gate and continue eventually passing through a third gate, still keeping to the base of the North Downs. Shortly after the third gate ignore a bridleway joining from the left and continue ahead until you meet a large crossing track marked by red arrows, beside a Forestry Commission sign. Turn left on to this track to climb steeply uphill for what seems a considerable distance. Near the top you should turn right through a wooden fence on to a path running along the top of the hill marked by white acorns, the North Downs Way. This is part of the route we followed earlier. Just after joining this path go over the first stile on your right beside an iron gate and follow the path left along the top of the hillside. Keep as near to the top of the hill as possible, following the tree line on your left until it ends and then go over a stile on your left. Go diagonally right uphill heading just left of the church spire ahead.

On reaching the brow you will see a large wooden gate and stile ahead which you should cross to reach the car park, the starting point of our walk. Just before you do though, look back at the view across the Surrey Weald and appreciate its beauty as John Evelyn did all those years ago.

ACCOMMODATION

The White Horse (THF), Dorking. Tel: 0306 881138

Two miles from the walk, the hotel has a good restaurant and comfortable rooms especially in the older parts of the building. At the rear is a secluded open air heated swimming pool.

Crossways Farm, Abinger Hammer, Dorking. Tel: 0306 730173

One and three quarter miles from the walk, Crossways Farm is a Jacobean farmhouse, built in the early part of the 17th century. Its entrance is through a lovely walled garden up a stone flagged path. Inside a great oak staircase leads up to comfortable rooms. If you wish to continue the magic of the olde worlde villages you have explored on the walk, then Crossways is a must.

Youth Hostel, Tanners Hatch YHA, Polesden Lacey, Dorking. Tel: 0372 52528

Three quarters of a mile from the walk, Tanners Hatch is an isolated cottage (you can only reach it by foot). Situated in the woods of Ranmore Common, the hostel has no electricity so bring your own lighting. Camping is also permitted.

Youth Hostel, Holmbury St. Mary. Tel: 0306 730777

Half a mile from the walk, a purpose built youth hostel set in large attractive grounds. The setting is superb, take one step out of the grounds and you are in the extensive Hurtwood. The youth hostel can be busy in summer with school parties - so be warned. Camping is permitted in the grounds.

Camping, Polesden Lacey, Dorking. Tel: 0372 456844

One and a half miles from the walk, this is a Camping and Caravanning Club site in a beautiful setting on an old cricket pitch in the grounds of Polesden Lacey, N.T. Please note that only tents and trailer tents are permitted.

BREACHING THE BORDER

Distance: 13 miles (21 km)

Time: Allow approximately 6 hours

Map: Ordnance Survey Landranger Map 187

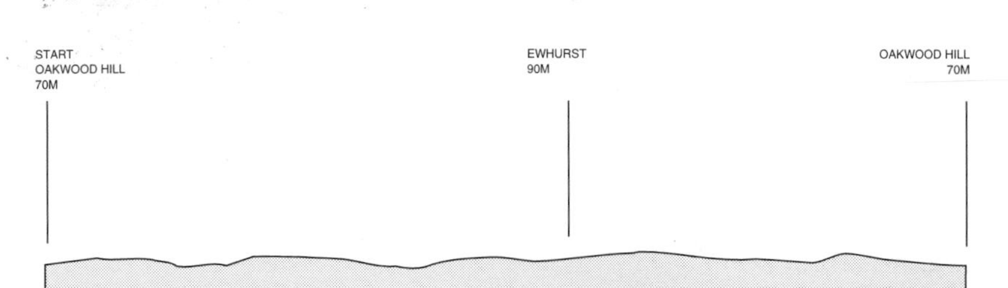

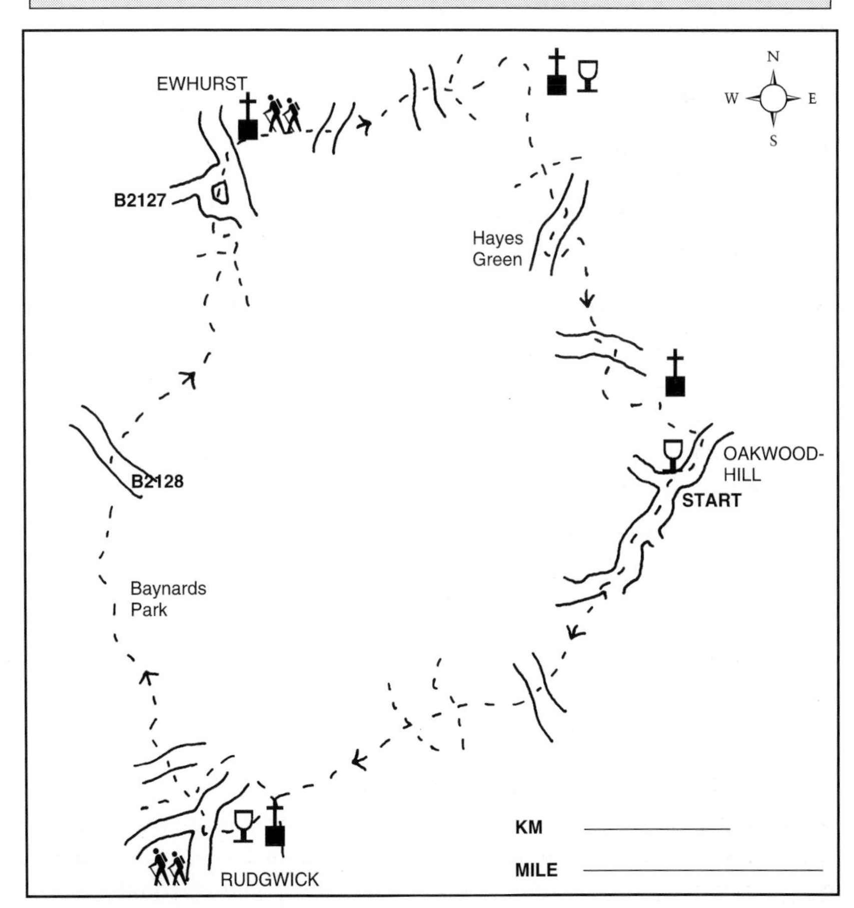

Walk Summary

Breaching the Border follows some of the lesser known paths in Surrey. Part of the walk follows the Surrey Sussex Border and the Sussex Border Path. Otherwise, the route is made up of minor footpaths and bridleways. The walk is a lowland one and therefore, not particularly strenuous and the paths are not as muddy as those nearer the North Downs, so you can if you want to risk it, get away with lighter footwear. One warning though, the paths being relatively less popular means that they can become overgrown in summer. Think twice before wearing shorts!

Start - OS. 133375 Map 187

The walk starts opposite "The Punchbowl" pub at Oakwood Hill. To get there take the A29 and then take the road west signposted to Oakwood Hill, one and a quarter miles south of Ockley. Alternative starting points are Ewhurst (OS. 093402 Map 187) and Rudgwick (OS. 091343 Map 187).

BREACHING THE BORDER

The walk starts opposite "The Punchbowl" pub. "The Punchbowl", a freehouse, is an excellent village pub with oak beams and a floor of huge flagstones. The pub serves a good range of real ales and compliments them with well prepared home cooked food. It is a good incentive to start the walk early in time to return before lunchtime closing.

Facing the pub, turn left and walk along the road ignoring a turning on your right skirting Oakwood Hill Cricket Club. Follow the road for three quarters of a mile until shortly after passing "Monks Tower", an unusual house on the left, take the footpath on the left beside "North Lodge". Do not make the mistake of turning left on to the drive, Monks Lane.

The footpath passes by the side of "North Lodge" and past a newly built property on your left. It then runs in a straight line between laurel bushes and you will soon see signs informing you that you are now on the Sussex Border Path. Ignore all crossing tracks to eventually arrive at a large house, "Honeywood House".

Follow the path through the grounds of the property following the signs, which lead you out to the gatehouse and a road. Cross the road and continue straight ahead along a concrete drive, still on the Sussex Border Path, heading for "Ridge Farm" to pass through the farm following the signs. Stay on the drive looking out for a lake in the distance on your left, this is in fact two reservoirs.

At another farm, "Bury St. Austens", you again carry straight on with the farmhouse on your left, keeping to the concrete drive. After half a mile, you will meet the high fencing of a deer farm and an equally high gate. Turn right here keeping the fence on your left and a field on your right, heading towards a white house at the far left corner of the field to go over a stile on to a drive way.

Cross the drive way passing the house on your left and a small pond on your right, leaving the Sussex Border Path which turns left, to continue straight ahead along another drive way. Follow the drive which curves gently left. Ignore a stile on your right to take a path on your right shortly after, rejoining the Sussex Border Path. Go across the field keeping to the right hand perimeter and pass through a gate to the right of a bungalow, "Highcroft Cottage".

Carry on along the edge of the property, passing through another gate and follow a drive until you see a Sussex Border Path sign pointing right. Turn right in the direction of the sign, passing through a kissing gate to cross a small field making for the church ahead. Pass through another kissing gate on to a fenced path and continue to pass through a third kissing gate into the church yard of The Holy Trinity, Rudgwick.

The Holy Trinity Church, Rudgwick (OS. 092344 Map 187). *This beautiful church dates from the 13th century. The squat west tower supported by huge buttresses is the only surviving part of the church*

from that century, the rest of the building being mainly 14th century. Of particular interest are a series of 14th century windows in the nave and isle. They are especially good examples of work from that period. The name Rudgwick is derived from ridge, after the ridge on which the church stands. Part of the church yard wall forms the boundary of Surrey and Sussex.

Go through the church yard following the gravel path to come out at a road beside "The Kings Head" pub, a Whitbread pub which serves good food. Cross the road in front of the pub and turn right heading north. Shortly after passing a road on your left, Lynwick Street, take a signposted public footpath left opposite some modern houses. The footpath which is fenced, runs between houses.

Ignore a stile on the right and continue to reach two stiles, the left being the Sussex Border Path. Cross the right hand stile and turn immediately left to follow the left hand perimeter of a field to reach and cross another stile on your left. Follow the footpath ahead with a hedge on your right and fencing on your left to pass "Maybanks Manor House" on your right.

The fenced path then leads down to a lane which you should cross and go over the stile ahead of you. Follow the right hand perimeter of the field passing a pond on your right and noting the circular ditch on your left, the remains of a moat. At the far corner of the field, cross the stile and continue along the right hand perimeter of the next field following the oak trees as they curve round. Cross another stile and carry straight on still keeping to the right hand perimeter of a field.

At top of the ridge go diagonally left across the field to the corner of the woods ahead, to cross a stile and enter the woods. Continue through the woods, Grub Copse, and on emerging turn left to meet a drive way. This is called Linarce Drive and leads to "Baynards Park". In front of you another drive joins at an angle. At the junction a narrow footpath leads off to the west through trees which you must take, this can be quite hidden in summer so take care not to miss it.

Follow the path passing behind a house between bushes, keeping in the direction of the yellow footpath arrows and passing to the right of chicken wire fencing. The path comes out into fields and bends round to the right hugging the side of a wood. There are good views here to your left across fields to "Collins Farm". Follow the path to cross a stile into the grounds of "Baynards Park", with the main tower of the house visible above the trees ahead of you.

i ***Baynards Park (OS. 086369 Map 187).*** *The name "Baynards" is after William Baynards who was given the land by William the Conqueror.*

The first records of a house here are in 1447, when it belong to Sir William Sidney. The current house was built by Sir George More, of Loseley around 1857. Its design is in fact based on the original "Loseley House". The house has the distinction that in its time it has been owned by four of the leading families of Surrey, namely the More's, the Bray's of Shere, the Evelyn's and the Onslow's. The house is believed to be haunted by Sir Thomas More, his wife, Margaret Roper, brought his head to the house keeping it in his favourite chest. It was eventually buried in the family vault at St. Dunstans, Canterbury. The ghost of "Baynards" and the ghost of "Loseley" are said to visit each other on alternate years.

Continue across the park heading to the right of a recently created pond ahead. Skirt the pond crossing a stream by a small footbridge and veer left to meet a drive beside some farm buildings, "Home Farm". Turn right and follow the drive around to the left passing to the left of the farm buildings and two houses on your right thereafter.

The drive continues ahead over another stream via a wooden bridge. Ignore the first drive way on the left, signposted as a bridleway, and when the drive way forks shortly after take the left hand drive, which is a dirt track, heading gently uphill through woodland. The track comes out at a road beside an old disused gatehouse to "Baynards Park". Cross the road and join the track ahead which runs along the top of Longhurst Hill, behind you and to your right are superb views of the surrounding countryside.

The track winds through woodland for approximately three quarters of a mile. You must look out for a stile on your left shortly after passing a gate on the same side. Go over the stile and follow a wide grass track downhill to cross another stile beside a cricket pavilion which from behind looks like a barn. Continue along a fenced path between the cricket pitch on your left and an attractive garden on your right, belonging to an equally attractive property, "Old House".

Follow the path, which is well signposted, through a small wooden gate and over a wooden bridge passing a series of ponds frequented by waterfowl on your right. Keep to the path which is fenced, to cross a stile into open parkland and follow the footpath to the drive way on to which you should turn left. There are good views ahead of the Surrey hills. Continue on the drive way to a cattle grid after which you should turn left along a signposted public footpath.

At a stile on your left turn right instead, to follow a small footpath through the woods and cross a stile into a field. Cross the field along a well marked path to reach a road beside a house which obviously belongs to a railway enthusiast. Go over a stile and cross the road to take a footpath beside the house opposite. This then runs between gardens to enter a modern close. Go along the road and as this bends round to the right, look out for a signposted public footpath on the left between conifers. Take this to arrive at a main road, the B2127. Turn right and follow the road round to the left. You are now in Ewhurst.

Ewhurst (OS. 093402 Map 187), *like the villages on the higher ground of Leith Hill, used to be renowned for vagabonds and smugglers. It was not even unusual for undesirables to be sent here to work out their sentences. Australia later took over this unfortunate role. Having the reputation of being an undesirable place, meant that Ewhurst and the surrounding area were often neglected, including the roads which gained the reputation of being some of the worst in the country. Cobbett described the roads as "bottomless" and the Prince of Denmark when travelling this way in 1703, commented "we did not get out of the coaches save when we were overturned or stuck".*

The village of Ewhurst today is attractive if not particularly beautiful. The church, which is off the main road, is worth a visit. This had to be largely rebuilt after an accident in 1839, which demolished most of the building. Of particular interest are the alter rails, they came originally from "Baynards Park", which explains their grand design. For the uninitiated, the original purpose of alter rails was to protect the alter from animals. In the early days, much of the population had to be bullied to go to church, often under threat of gaol or a fine. These people, who were in the main peasants, would bring their livelihood to church with them, turning the church into a grand farm yard. You can immediately understand why alter rails became necessary.

For refreshments there is "The Bull's Head" pub (Friary Meux), as well a shop selling a wide range of provisions.

Immediately after a pond beside a bus stop turn right along a track marked as a public footpath, passing bungalows on your right. As the drive way continues down to a private house, veer left staying on the public footpath. On reaching a field ahead, turn right along a well trodden path and ignore a turning off to your left shortly after, to continue straight on. Sometime after look out for another turning left, which you should take, crossing a stream via a small bridge.

Go across a field along a fenced path to cross a stile beside a wooden gate and follow a grass track with farm buildings on your right to reach a lane. Turn left and walk along the lane and after approximately 100 metres, turn right going over a stile into a field. Follow the left hand perimeter of the field to the far left hand corner. Cross another stile and go over a small wooden bridge and over a third stile into a field. Go straight ahead to the right of a large house, "North Bridge Manor". Pass a tennis court on your left following the perimeter fencing of the property and continue straight on to the other side of the field to cross a stile.

Follow the fenced path ahead to come out at a lane opposite "Cobbetts Farm". Cross the lane to go over a stile into a field and continue straight on keeping to the left hand perimeter. As the field perimeter bears left, you should leave this to continue straight on to go between two ponds and thereafter follow the perimeter of the pond on your left to meet the edge of a wood. continue straight on following the perimeter

Go over the stile and head for the left hand corner of the next field. At the far side of the field, go over another stile across a narrow strip of woodland and over a third stile into another field. Ahead of you is "Waterland Farm" and in the distance Leith Hill. Follow the left hand perimeter of this field to cross a stile beside a farm gate and continue ahead to the far left hand corner of the next field, where you cross two stiles either side of a wooden plank bridge.

Turn right after the bridge and go over a stile which is ten paces away. Turn right immediately after the stile and follow the perimeter of the field for approximately 50 paces to go over another stile and continue ahead, keeping to the right hand perimeter of a field.

Shortly, you will see through a gap in some trees ahead to your left, the small brick church of Forest Green. Turn right at the first stile you come to unless you wish to visit Forest Green, in which case you should take the second stile a short distance further on and follow the path across fields to the village. Forest Green is an attractive village set around a large village green, which houses a cricket pitch and village pond. The village pub, "The Parrot", (Courage), has its own Parrot beer and serves a wide range of food. The church visible from our route, is also worth a visit.

To continue our route, go over the first stile across a stream via a wooden bridge and go over another stile on to the drive to "Waterland Farm". Turn left along the drive way and after a short distance, turn right on to a wide grass track. Follow this as it bends round to the right and cross the stile at the end, to the left of a farm gate.

Turn left and continue along the left hand perimeter of the field, at the end of which you should cross the stile into the next field and cross this, going diagonally right to the corner. There are good views at this point behind you of Leith Hill and Leith Hill Tower. Go through a gate into the next field and continue across to the right hand corner, cross a stile and continue diagonally left to the corner of another field. Pass through a metal gate and continue along the left hand side of the field to pass through a wooden gate on to a tarmac lane, Pond Head Lane, beside a particularly attractive farmhouse.

Cross the lane and go over a stile by some outbuildings and continue across a field to cross a second stile and a second field. At the other side, go over two stiles and continue straight across the field ahead descending into a valley to a stream. Go over a bridge and continue steeply up the other side to go across a field heading for a metal gate. Pass through the gate and turn right along the lane passing a beautiful half timber cottage on your left to reach the small hamlet of Mayes Green.

Take the track on the left at the far side of the green and follow this for approximately a quarter of a mile, to turn right on to another track, Green Lane, a public bridleway. The track passes a golf course on your left before reaching a tarmac road, which you should join and continue straight ahead. The road ends at a "T" junction with "Okewood Cottage" on your right. Turn left and continue along the road for a short distance and just before the entrance to "The Gatton Manor Hotel", turn right along a small somewhat hidden footpath through the woods. Take care not to miss this.

The footpath winds through the woods with fencing on the left to cross two stiles, one after the other, passing through a cottage garden. Continue straight on entering woods to cross another stile and follow the right hand perimeter of a field. At the right hand corner of the field, go over a stile and follow the path left descending gently into a pretty wooded valley. After crossing a bridge, turn left and shortly after fork right to cross another bridge and continue on up to the church yard of Okewood Church.

Okewood Church (OS. 128381 Map 187), *as well as being the most remote in Surrey, must also be one of the prettiest. We are indeed fortunate that the church is here at all for its history has been one of survival. It was built in 1220 as a simple chapel on a site which originally housed a Roman villa and before that, a Druid temple. In 1431, one Edward de la Hale, donated £200 for improvements to the chapel. This was his way of thanking God after his son had narrowly escaped death from a wild boar whilst out hunting in the surrounding woodland. There is a brass memorial in the church to Edward de la Hale.*

In 1547, Edward VI, passed an Act of Parliament dissolving unofficial places of worship. Mistakenly, Okewood Chapel, was regarded as a chantry chapel and was seized by the Crown. The chapel became redundant but the local people refused to give up their right to prayer and petitioned Parliament. Their argument was finally heard and in 1553, it was agreed that the chapel would be officially recognised and restored to the parish. Unfortunately, before all this could happen, King Edward died and with the troubled accession of Queen Mary, the decree was forgotten.

It was not until 1560, during the reign of Queen Elizabeth I, that the chapel was finally restored to the parish and a priest once more appointed. However, the land belonging to the chapel was never returned and the chapel had to survive on donations for its existence. The chapel's future was not finally secured until 1853, when it became Okewood Church.

Follow the path passing to the right of the church and leave the churchyard via a small wooden gate. After a short distance turn left (do not follow the path right), to walk through the woods. After some time look out for a path on your right, which you should take to continue through a hazel coppice, later crossing a small stream. Soon after you will pass fields on your right and thereafter a large gate post. The path arrives at a road on to which you should turn right. Follow the road round until you reach your starting point at "The Punchbowl".

ACCOMMODATION

Kings Arms, Ockley. Tel: 0306 711224

Two miles from the walk, the Kings Arms is a three hundred year old inn, which has kept its traditional character with many original features. The inn has a separate restaurant which is very comfortable and a large childrens room. The bedrooms are well furnished and have good views.

Bulmer Farm, Holmbury St. Mary. Tel: 0306 730210

Three miles from the walk, Bulmer Farm is a lovely 17th century farmhouse offering first class accommodation at very reasonable prices. Guests can enjoy a lovely beamed lounge with log fires in winter and a large well planned garden.

Youth Hostel, Holmbury St. Mary YHA. Tel:0306 730777

Four and a half miles from the walk, a purpose built youth hostel set in large attractive grounds. The setting is superb, take one step out of the grounds and you are in the extensive Hurtwood. The youth hostel can be busy in summer with school parties - so be warned. Camping is permitted in the grounds.

THE HAMBLEDON FLIGHT

Distance: 13¼ miles (21.2 km)

Time: Allow approximately 6½ hours

Map: Ordnance Survey Landranger Map 186

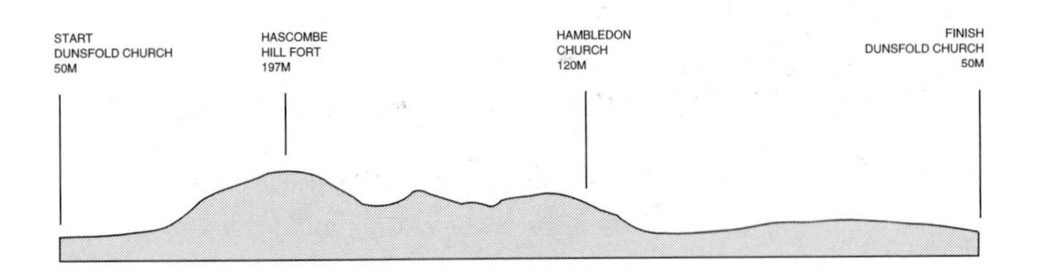

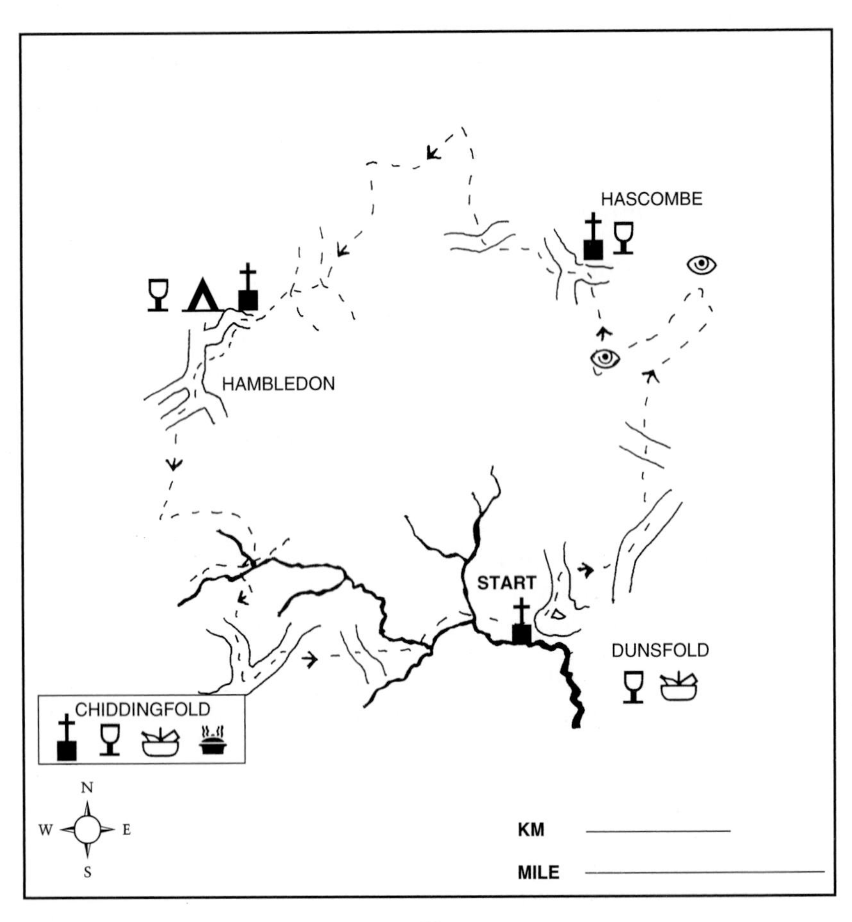

Walk Summary

The Hambledon Flight passes through some of the most picturesque and unspoilt villages in Surrey. It also takes in Hambledon Hurst, a still impressive wood which was once part of the great forest of the Surrey Weald. The going can be very muddy especially in Hambledon Hurst and the hills are a lot harder than they at first appear.

Start - OS. 998364 Map 186

The walk starts from Dunsfold church which is signposted from the village of Dunsfold. Dunsfold village is just off of the B2130 from Godalming. Another recommended starting point is the church at Hambledon (OS. 971390 Map 186).

THE HAMBLEDON FLIGHT

Your starting point is Dunsfold church.

Dunsfold church (OS. 999364 Map 186) *set some distance from the village, was built in the 13th century. It was something of an experiment in its time and became the forerunner of a design later used throughout the country. The benches in the church nave are the earliest surviving in Britain and still have holes to take the candle holders. In the church yard stands a yew reputed to be over 1000 years old, now supported by an intricate pattern of wires and stakes. The church yard also has one of the few remaining holy wells in the country. One mystery surrounds the church, it is said that the church plate was buried to avoid being seized during the reformation. Its existence and location still remain undiscovered.*

Leaving the church yard, take the left hand lane passing "Church Green House" and "Larks Rise" on your left. Continue along the lane until it meets a "T" junction, at which point turn left and go along the lane looking out for a bridleway signposted on your right. Cross over a stile beside an iron gate and continue ahead, keeping to the right of the hedge in front of you. Head for a wooden gate in the left hand corner of the field and pass through entering into a narrow hazel wooded valley. The path then continues down hill, crossing over a stream and up the other side of the valley. At the top you reach another stile which you go over into a field and continue straight ahead towards a house. On reaching the right hand corner of the field, cross another stile arriving at the large village green of Dunsfold.

Ahead of you is one of the many village ponds frequented by well fed, but forever hungry ducks. For refreshments and Dunsfold village centre, turn right to follow the main road into the village.

Dunsfold (OS. 007363 Map 186) *was once surrounded by the great forest of the Surrey Weald, known in Roman times as Anderida Silva. The fold in Dunsfold is the old Saxon name for an enclosure in a forest. The current village has no real centre the houses are scattered like seeds thrown from a farmer's hand. Most of the houses cling loosely to a large village green, which is home for several small ponds which in turn are home to a variety of fish and waterfowl. If visiting one of the village pubs, it is not uncommon to be followed by a line of hungry ducks. In recent times, the village has been home to a nearby airfield, a village pub once called "The Hawk and Harrier" reflected the association. Today the two pubs are "Rumpoles", a free house with a restaurant and "The Sun Inn", Friary Meux, also with a restaurant. There is also a Village Stores which doubles as a Post Office where you can buy a wide range of refreshments.*

To continue our walk, turn left passing between the duck pond and cottages on your left. At the second pond on the green, continue straight on keeping the houses on your left and the main road on your right. Follow the main road until shortly after the last building on your left and almost opposite the entrance sign to Dunsfold, you reach a somewhat hidden footpath on your left - take care not to miss it. Go over a stile into a field and take a diagonal right across the field, heading for the last tree on the right of a line of scotch pines. At this point cross another stile, cross the drive leading to "Park Farm", and then over a second stile into a large open field. From here there are good views ahead of Hascombe Hill and a reminder that the more strenuous stretches of the walk are still to come!

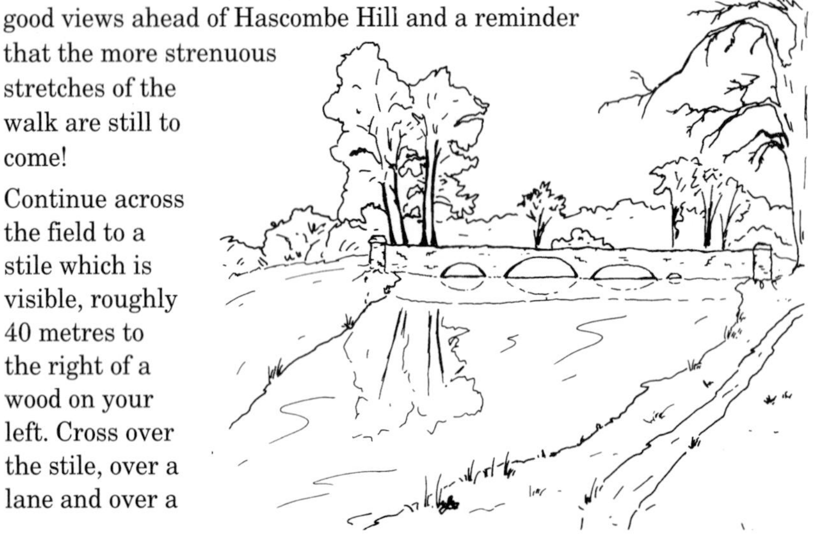

Continue across the field to a stile which is visible, roughly 40 metres to the right of a wood on your left. Cross over the stile, over a lane and over a second stile into another field. Just ahead of you is a stone arched ornamental dam. You should pass to the left of this and continue alongside a small oval pond created by the dam. At the far end of the field just beyond the far reaches of the pond, you will reach another stile beside a farm gate. Go over the stile and continue straight ahead uphill along a drive.

When the drive bends sharply to the left, you turn off to the right onto the concrete forecourt of a barn and pass through an iron gate, following the yellow arrow to reach and cross a stile ahead of you. Continue straight on, keeping the barn on your right, to a post again displaying the yellow arrow. Follow the direction of the arrow along a reasonable path to the brow of the hill and then over another stile into another field, which has been left to grow wild.

The path continues ahead along the right hand perimeter of the field, with good views across the Surrey Weald on your right. This part of the walk can be quite tough going, especially if the bracken is at its height, but the path is fairly regularly used and easy to define. As a point of interest, the large field to the right has every time I have walked this route contained an unusual breed of pig. I don't know if they belong to the farm below, "Grubbins Farm", but if they do it is appropriately named. At the end of the field, go over a stile and through an iron gate, following the path through fairly dense scrub where blackberries and elderberries are in abundance. As the scrub thins out you continue through woodland and after a short time, you will pass a large house, "Nore House", on your right with a well manicured garden. The path continues between the house and a tennis court and immediately thereafter, you should turn left on to a track signposted as a bridleway, opposite a large iron gate to the property. Do not make the mistake of taking the second track on your left. The track progresses steeply uphill with good views on your right of the North Downs.

On reaching the top of the ridge (you are not at the top of the hill yet), which affords yet more good views, take a smaller fairly undefined path on your left. This winds its way up through beech woods becoming more prominent as it progresses. The beech trees change to sweet chestnuts and then thin out, allowing the best views yet across the Surrey Weald to Leith Hill and the South Downs. The path follows the perimeter of Hascombe Hill for a considerable distance and at one point a path from the left joins it. You should continue straight on. If you have sharp eyes, it is possible to re-trace your route below. You eventually meet steep banks on your right which are the remains of an iron age hill fort.

Hascombe Hill hill fort 197m/644ft (OS. 004386 Map 186). *At the* *summit of Hascombe Hill sits an iron age hill fort still recognisable today by the steep banks which remain as a testament to their builders' efforts. The views from here are spectacular and the hill must have been a superb place to live. Hascombe Hill is the highest hill in the area and in the early 19th century was an important telegraph station, a link in a chain of telegraph stations sending signals from the Admiralty in London to the dockyards in Portsmouth.*

The path follows the steep banks of the fort for some distance still along the perimeter of the hill, with excellent views to your left of Hurt Wood and "Raswell" a large white property. Follow the path as it turns left away from the hill fort and commence your descent between rhododendron bushes, the path becoming progressively steeper as you go. When the path turns sharply to the left, ignore this and leave the path to continue straight on, following a much narrower path - take care not to miss this. Veer right on to a more defined path running between steep banks and continue straight on to cross a stile ahead of you behind a small wooden garage. You will come out into a small lane, turn left proceeding downhill to reach "The White Horse" pub, a 16th century free house with a large beer garden. The pub has an excellent reputation for food and in the summer often has a barbecue which can be very popular. It is worth making time to visit the village of Hascombe and to do this, pass in front of the pub and follow Church Road.

Hascombe village (OS. 002397 Map 186) *lies cut off from the outside world at the bottom of a dead-end lane. Its position has allowed it to retain its character and today the village remains as it has for many years. Like all good villages Hascombe has a village pond on which there are a variety of ducks. It also has some lovely cottages and a church which is younger than it appears. The church visible today was built in 1863 at a cost of £3,100. It is a wonderful example of what the Victorians could do to recreate an earlier style of building. One person of note who lived in Hascombe, is Nicholas Hussey who was Sheriff of Surrey and Sussex during the reign of Henry VI whom he served.*

Our route continues crossing the road in front of the pub and over a stile opposite into a field which you should cross. You are now on the Greensand Way, "GW". Do not cross the stile at the other side of the field, but turn right immediately in front of it and continue along the edge of the field until you come to a gate. Pass through the gate and continue straight on until the path forks, at which point you should take the right hand path.

On reaching a tarmac drive, turn right and then almost immediately left along a wooden hand-railed path marked as a public footpath. This leads to the outbuildings of a large and very attractive property, "Hoe Farm", where you should cross another stile, continuing between the house and tennis court, passing a pond on your left to cross a second stile. Continue ahead towards the left hand corner of the field, cross a stile turning immediately right and after approximately 25 paces, cross another stile on to a small path which leads uphill through woodland. As you near the top, follow the path round to the left and continue straight on through Foxbury Copse, ignoring all minor joining paths.

When the path bends right take the left fork straight ahead which may appear less prominent, until you reach a large dirt track. Turn right on to the track and continue downhill to a narrow lane which you should cross, to join another well used track signposted as a bridleway.

Shortly after passing through a narrow gate beside a larger one, the track becomes tarmacced and passes between some rather grand properties. One which particularly stands out is "Hascombe Court", on your right.

Follow the track, though it should now be called a lane, to its end ignoring all turnings off. The lane ends when it meets another road on a bend. Do not join the road, but turn left passing in front of a post box and continue down a tarmacced drive, signposted to "High Barn" and "Bridle Cottage". As the drive bends left into "High Barn", you continue straight on along a track marked "Bridle Track only to Hydon". The track follows the perimeter of "High Barn" which has some impressive gardens and leads downhill to cross an attractive fielded valley. It continues up over a rise for some distance, before dropping steeply into another this time wooded valley, Juniper Valley. At this point a path joins our route from the left. Take this, almost going back on yourself and uphill. Are the legs beginning to ache?

Passing through a sweet chestnut coppice, ignore the turning off to the right and continue straight on, following the path as it bends right when it reaches the perimeter of a field. Continue until you meet a road. Note the change in soil along this path which is now almost completely sand. Cross the road and follow a narrow path marked public bridleway. You are now traversing Hydon Heath where the path continues through more chestnut coppices. The path then cuts through a shallow bank which could have been an old wall and perhaps a boundary. It then meets another path coming in from the right and continues straight on descending gently through more mature woodland. Ignore all crossing and joining tracks until you meet a junction of tracks at the edge of some fields. Veer right, ignoring the two paths on your left, keeping the field on your left and a chestnut coppice on your right.

At the next junction of tracks continue straight on along a narrow path, which almost immediately joins a wider track. Continue ahead on this for a short distance until you meet yet another junction, this time beside a small brick building which belongs to Thames Water and is Hydon's Ball booster station. If you have the energy, the path on your right leads you uphill to Hydon's Ball.

Hydon's Ball 179m/593ft and Hydon's Heath (OS. 978396 Map 186). *Hydon's Heath is over 100 acres of heath and woodland under the care of the National Trust. The highest point is Hydon's Ball which has a small memorial with an inscription "On Hydon's top there is a cup and in that cup there is a drop. Take up the cup and drink the drop and place the cup on Hydon's top". If you climb to the top of Hydon's Ball on a hot day you will probably need a drop out of Hydon's cup. If you cannot find the cup however, the view is reward enough.*

Our route however, is straight ahead passing the booster station on your left. After a short distance, turn left beside an old disused barn and follow the path to pass through a kissing gate into a large field. Cross the field diagonally by way of a well used path, heading for a large oak tree. Pass through another kissing gate and continue towards Hambledon church which is now in view.

Pass through yet another gate to the left of the church yard and continue ahead passing some old lime kilns on your left. The church is well worth a visit as is the "Merry Harriers" pub, Friary Meux, which is reached by taking the grass path which forks right by "Stable Cottage" gate and continues downhill to the pub. The pub which is 16th century comes complete with inglenook fireplace and chamber pots hanging from the beamed ceiling. Hikers are welcome and you are even allowed to eat your own sandwiches though the pub food is worth tasting. You can also camp on the green opposite.

Hambledon church (OS. 971390 Map 186) and Hambledon village (OS. 967385 Map 186). *Hambledon more than most Surrey villages, reflects the days gone by. Several of its cottages belong to the National Trust (not open to the public) and nearly all the rest are protected. Eric Parker, author of Highways and Byeways in Surrey, fittingly made his home here. The village church, St. Peter's, is particularly pretty and sits beside some equally attractive properties. In its church yard is a hollow yew tree, said to be able to house twelve* *people in its trunk. Legend has it that if you walk three times round the inside of the trunk, you will see a witch - dare you try it?*

From Hambledon church continue along the lane taking the first footpath on the left (not the second), opposite the entrance to "Court Farm". Go over a stile, marked with a yellow arrow engraved with "GW" (the Greensand Way) and cross the field on a diagonal path to reach another stile. The view from this field is of Black Down (280m).

Crossing over the stile, go diagonally across the next field, bearing away from the houses on your right until you reach the far corner and another stile. At this point you will have good views ahead of the South Downs and behind you of St. Peter's church. Cross the stile and go steeply downhill, passing a modern house on your left.

The path reaches a lane beside a house, "Mattyers", pass the front of the house and immediately after, take the public bridleway on your left. Running between two tall banks, the bridleway leads you to a small village green where you should veer right and continue until you reach the road. Cross the road on to a track, signposted to "Beech Cottage". Directly in front of the cottage, take the footpath on your left which leads downhill away from the village.

On reaching a road, cross over, turn right and continue down a gravel drive on your left, in front of a large house. If in doubt, look out for a public bridleway sign opposite the original path. The drive leads to "Good Brook Stables" where you should continue straight on along a narrow footpath. This path meets a wider track in front of a large pond, at which point you should turn left. After passing a cottage on your left, the path plunges deep into Hambledon Hurst. Hambledon Hurst is all that remains of the woodland that dominated this area.

The path that you follow is the original highway between Godalming and Chiddingfold. Going by local records, the path is not in any better repair today than it was in the 15th and 16th centuries. Continue along the path through the wood on an almost perfectly straight line south for approximately three quarters of a mile. The path twists only twice once left over a stream and later on to the right by way of a more prominent crossing.

When the path begins to climb very gradually uphill, you should look out for a fenced field on your right often used as a lorry park, known locally as Cuckoo Corner. Just before the field albeit almost opposite, turn left on to a smaller path taking care not to miss it. If you find yourself walking straight on with a field on your right, you should back track to find the turning.

This smaller path twists through the wood, which by now can give the feeling of being everlasting and gives us some idea of what it must have been like a few hundred years ago, when Hambledon Hurst covered hundreds of square miles instead of acres. Look out for a patchwork of banks on your right which are old field boundaries. At a fork, turn right and follow the meandering path through the wood until you reach another fork at which you should go right again (ignore a path on your right immediately before the fork), now following a much wider path. Almost thankfully you meet a field on your left, but the path bears right again, back into the depths of Hambledon Hurst.

As a marker, another field will shortly appear on your left, you should continue straight on along the same path. After some time, the path descends and as the valley bottoms out you reach a "T" junction at which you should turn right and go over a small wooden-planked bridge, continuing straight on to meet a stream on your left. Continue on to reach a public bridleway sign and turn left crossing the stream by way of a larger wooden bridge. On the other side you will find yourself on a gravel based track leading uphill.

Nearing the top of the hill the path breaks out of the wood and the view is of open fields and a large house on your left "Stonehurst". Follow the path which is fenced until you reach the drive way to "Stonehurst". Cross the drive and go over a stile marked public bridleway, into a field keeping to the left hand perimeter. Leave the field by another stile adjacent to a picturesque property, "Yew Tree Cottage", and continue ahead along a wide track until you reach a lane beside some farm buildings. At this point, continue left along the lane, passing "Ryestead" on your right until you reach a "T" junction in front of "Ryestead House". If you are not too tired turn right here to visit Chiddingfold.

i

Chiddingfold (OS. 963355 Map 186). *This attractive village comes complete with village pond, village green, a working forge and in my opinion the best inn in the country, the 13th century "Crown Inn". The "Crown Inn" was built as a guest house for travelling pilgrims and Cistercian monks in 1258 and has since accommodated King Edward VI and Queen Elizabeth I. Up until the reign of Elizabeth I, Chiddingfold was a famous glass making centre including stained glass the most notable of which can be seen in Westminster Abbey and St. George's Chapel, Windsor. Chiddingfold was also well known for producing iron and many hammer ponds still remain.*

Today, Chiddingfold has one of the few walking stick works in the country. It is also home to an excellent summer village fair and in November, has one of the best village bonfires in Surrey. After a drink and perhaps lunch at the Crown Inn, retrace your steps to where you left the original route.

If Chiddingfold seems too far to stray and all you can imagine is a hot bath, then turn left instead to continue our walk. After approximately 300 metres along the lane, turn right on to a wide gravel track leading into the woods signposted as a public bridleway. The bridleway very quickly leaves the woods to run between shallow banks with fields either side.

At the top of the rise on your left, once stood a Roman villa. Like the iron age fort earlier in our walk thoughtfully positioned, though for different reasons. The bridleway comes out beside "White Beech Cottage" on your left. Turn right along the lane and after a few paces turn left into the drive way of "White Beech Farm", passing in front of the property to go between two posts with a barn on your right.

Continue along a footpath to the left of a field, which is fenced. At the far end of the field the path enters an area of particularly attractive woodland, Duns Copse, and winds on for some time to cross a stream by way of a concrete bridge. After this the path bends right and follows the stream in an easterly direction. The path constantly meets the stream along the way and you could do a lot worse than to take a rest along its banks or even to cool your feet in its waters. The path eventually leaves the wood via a wooden gate into a field.

Walk across the field to meet the left hand perimeter and then follow the perimeter fencing until you reach a wide track leading off to your left (this may be fenced off but is designed to be easily opened). Do not go up this track but go over a wooden fence which acts as a stile, immediately on the right hand side of the track. Continue along a narrow path still on the left hand perimeter of the field, but on the other side of the fence.

Pass through an iron gate into a small field, keeping to the right of the field until you pass through a five bar farm gate, into a field which doubles as a farm yard. When I last walked this route the farmer had tied an old tyre to a tree for children to use as a swing and on it he had painted "Hi" - a nice touch. Continue ahead to the right of the farm yard to come out in front of Dunsfold church with its lovely old yew entrance. You are now back at the starting point of our walk.

ACCOMMODATION

The Crown Inn, The Green, Chiddingfold. Tel: 0428 792255

One mile from the walk this is, in my view, the best inn in the country. Built in 1285, its rooms unlike most period hotels, genuinely feel as though they are from that age. If it is more than you would usually pay for accommodation then save up, its worth it.

Knipp Cottage, Pickhurst Road, Chiddingfold. Tel: 0428 682062

One mile from the walk, this is a beautiful house in a beautiful setting complete with tennis court and outdoor pool to relieve those tired feet.

Youth Hostel, Hindhead YHA, Devils Punchbowl, Hindhead. Tel: 0428 734285

Approximately nine miles from the walk, a simple youth hostel situated in the bowl of the Devils Punchbowl. Basic but idyllic and I loved it. Camping is also permitted.

Camping, The Merry Harriers pub, Hambledon Road, Hambledon. Tel: 0428 792883.

On the walk, one can camp on a green opposite the Merry Harriers pub. What more can you want!

HIGH CHART CHALLENGE

Distance: 14 miles (22.5 km)

Time: Allow approximately 6 hours

Map: Ordnance Survey Landranger Map 187

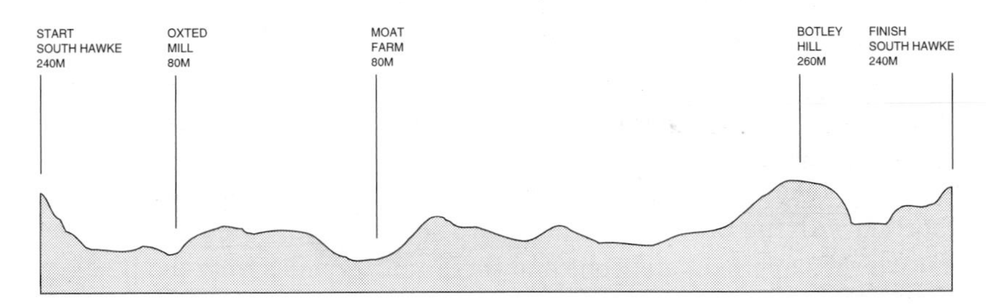

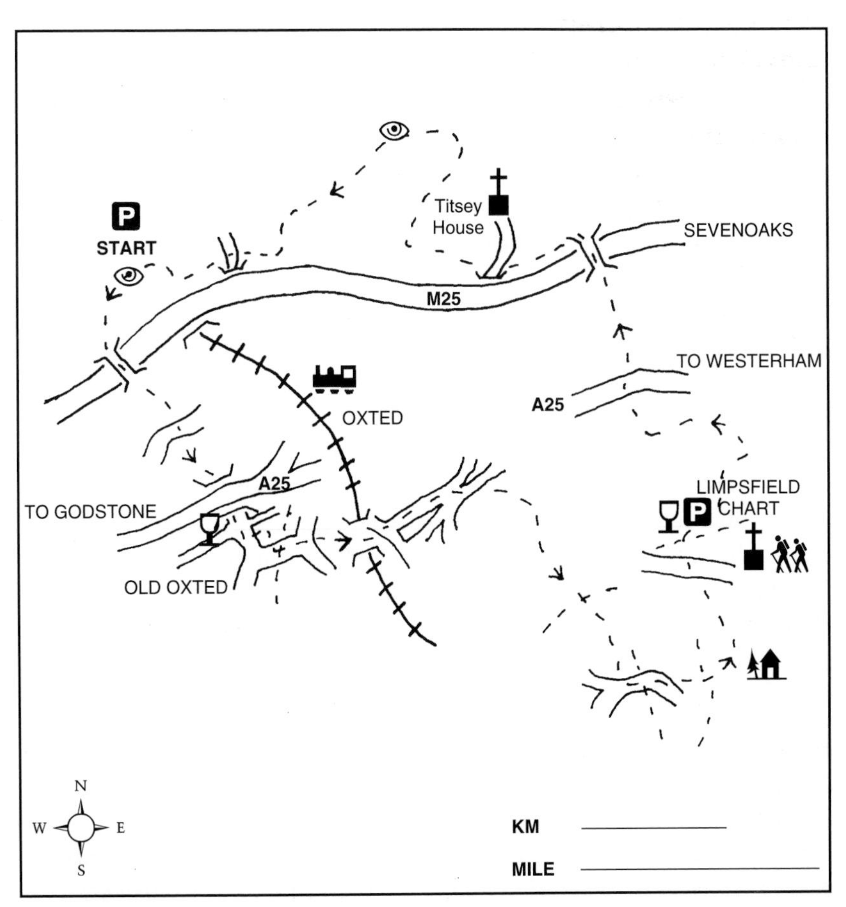

Walk Summary

The High Chart Challenge follows part of the North Downs and Greensand Ridge in the very east of Surrey. The longest walk in the book, the High Chart Challenge also has more ascents than any other and should not be tackled if you are unfit. Some of the climbs can be very slippery in wet weather as can some of the narrower paths skirting the North Downs. Unless you are prepared for a fall, good footwear is essential. As a reward for your effort, the route offers constant good views as well as a few local surprises.

Start - OS. 373541 Map 187

The walk starts from a car park at South Hawke on Tandridge Hill. To get there, take the road to Woldingham from the B269, just after the junction with the B2024 at Botley Hill. Then take the second road on the left which is approximately one and three quarter miles from the B269. The car park is on the right as the road bends sharply right, opposite an entrance to "South Hawke House".

If coming from Woldingham, take the road south out of the village and turn right as the road bends sharply left. This road leads to the car park opposite the entrance to "South Hawke House". Another good place to start is St. Andrew's Church, Limpsfield Chart (OS. 426518 Map 187), where there is a parking area. Oxted has a railway station and from there it is one mile to "Barrow Green Court" where you can join the walk.

THE HIGH CHART CHALLENGE

P From the car park cross the road and follow the signposted public footpath ahead down steps, to turn right along the North Downs Way. At the first wooden bench, which you should take care not to miss, take the small narrow path in front of the bench downhill to soon enter undergrowth. Ignore minor crossing and joining paths and follow the path, which can be slippery in wet weather, diagonally right downhill and at the bottom cross a stile into a field. Go straight across the field to join a more prominent track and cross a second stile. Follow the track via a bridge over the motorway, M25, and continue straight on along a gravel track through woodland to later pass a large property on your left, "Barrow Green Court".

i ***Barrow Green Court (OS. 380531 Map 187)*** *is a fine early 17th century Jacobean red brick building, first belonging to one Richard Monshurst. In the late 1 7th century, Charles Hoskin obtained the property and the Hoskin's coat of arms is much in evidence. There are many references to the Hoskin family at Oxted church, one particularly* *moving epitaph is that of Anne Hoskin who died in 1651. The epitaph tells of Anne being a "map of misery", meaning sadly that her body was riddled with disease. In the late 18th century, the Duke of Devonshire married Catherine Hoskin and made his home there.*

The house has remained in the Hoskin family until recently when it was purchased by a gentleman from the Middle East. It is now surrounded by high security fencing The name "Barrow Green" is derived from the large circular mound which you will shortly pass on the opposite side of the road. The mound is said to commemorate a battle with the Danes.

The gravel track then joins a tarmac drive to arrive at Barrow Green road with a beautiful Elizabethan farmhouse on your right, "Barrow Green Farm". Cross the road and pass through the kissing gate ahead to join a signposted public footpath going across a field. Go through another kissing gate, cross over a small stream and pass a small picturesque lake on your right.

Continue straight ahead passing sweet chestnut trees to go through a third kissing gate to reach a road beside a cottage, "The Lodge". Turn right along the road and continue, crossing over a stream and passing lovely period cottages. Go under the main road, the A25, up to Old Oxted, beside "The Old Bell", a pub and carvery.

Old Oxted (OS. 385523 Map 187), *separated from the new Oxted by the A25 which you have just passed under, is one long street, the original main road of half timbered houses. The street has several popular pubs. One of the oldest is "The Old Bell", which is 15th century and has a resident ghost. Lucy's Spirit, as the ghost is fondly known, is believed to be that of a chambermaid who hanged herself in one of the bedrooms.*

To continue our route, cross the road and go straight on up Beadles Lane to reach a school where you should turn left into Springfield. Leave the road as it bends round to the left to join a footpath ahead beside a large metal gate.

Follow the fenced footpath with a small field on your left and enter woodland running parallel with a stream, to meet a pond on your left set in a lovely garden belonging to "Willow Mere". The path brings you to a lane and "Oxted Mill".

Oxted Mill (OS. 390518 Map 187) *is actually two mills, the first being built in the mid-19th century, the second as late as the early 1890's. They were both fed by the river Eden, which was dammed to create the ponds you have just passed. Flour milling continued here right up until 1951, when the buildings were purchased by a car accessories firm.*

Turn left in front of the mill and go up the lane, Spring Lane, to meet another road. Cross the road, turn left and almost immediately right on to a footpath marked as the Greensand Way, "GW". Follow the footpath between gardens for approximately half a mile, ignoring paths off to your left and right, to reach a drive which leads into a rather smart road opposite "Icewood House". Turn left along the road to pass a number of large properties, "Limpsfield Court", being one of the grander and worth a second look.

On reaching a "T" junction, go straight across on to a signposted public bridleway and continue on to Limpsfield common. At this point, take the left fork ahead marked as a public bridleway and continue ignoring any joining and crossing paths. You will soon see houses on your left and the bridleway continues parallel to the lane adjacent to the houses. Stay on the bridleway until you reach a junction of footpaths, marked by a "Footpath" and "Horses" sign. Go straight ahead to the left of the sign (do not turn left) to twist through the wood and ultimately veer left to meet the lane mentioned earlier.

Turn right along the lane in front of a very impressive building, "St. Michael's School for Girls". On meeting a road, cross this to join the bridleway ahead, the Greensand Way, and follow this until you meet a junction of tracks where you should bear right to cross a lane ahead. Go into a parking area and take the public bridleway left, again marked as the Greensand Way, "GW". Ignore a left hand fork and continue on to the next fork at which you should veer right. Cross over a junction of paths and go uphill ignoring two separate crossing paths to reach a service road. At the service road, turn left to meet another road on to which you should turn right. Walk along the road and after passing the drive to "Links Cottage" on the left, take the footpath left and cross a golf tee to reach a road in front of "Pains Hill Chapel".

Cross the road and go over a stile to take the path to the left of the chapel between fences. This then arrives at another road where you should turn left and stay on the road until you meet a "T" junction in front of "Arden Cottage". Turn left to pass another cottage on your right with a sign on the wall commemorating a Russian, "Sercey Kravehinsky Stepniak".

Approximately 25 paces after the cottage, turn right along a path which can at first appear to be a path way to the cottage, almost going back on yourself. Follow the path passing the cottage again to go gradually downhill between banks. Cross over a stile into a field and cross the field heading for the far right hand corner. As you progress downhill take time to look at the view to your left, where a grand brick built property, "Chartlands", sits majestically on the Greensand Ridge. Leave the field via another stile beside a metal five bar gate and continue along the track ahead to pass to the right of the out buildings of a "Tenchley Manor Farm". The farmhouse is 16th century and sits beside the original road from Limpsfield to Edenbridge.

After the farm buildings turn right to go down the drive and after approximately 50 metres, look out for a path on your left marked by a yellow arrow on a wooden telegraph pole. Take this path, which can be undefined, to go over a small bridge into a field where you should turn right heading for the gate in front of you, keeping as a rough guide, to the left of the telegraph poles. Cross the stile beside the gate and turn left along a lane and continue until you reach a farmhouse opposite a small duck pond.

This is "Moat Farm", so called because it used to be surrounded by a moat, the duck pond now being all that remains. The house is 16th century and together with the pond, it creates one of those rare picturesque settings that are typically English. "Ducks Crossing" signs warn the walker that they might be hassled for food. Immediately after the last building by the pond, "The Old Lodge", turn left over a stile following the sign for a public footpath. Head for the top left hand corner of the field to cross a second stile and turn immediately right along the right hand perimeter of a field. Cross another stile and follow the left hand perimeter of the next field to a fourth stile which you should cross into a lane.

The stile ahead leads to Crockham Hill. To continue our walk however, go left along the lane, this being part of the Vanguard Way, heading for the Greensand Ridge. Pass some cottages on your left and "Treveux Manor" on your right. The lane, which turns into a track, bends left after the cottages and continues uphill for some distance to join a tarmac drive. Continue straight on passing some beautiful properties and as you near the top look for "The Old School" on the left, which has a large twin chimney doubling as a bell tower.

On meeting a road cross this to join another road straight ahead following the signs to "The Carpenter's Arms", to pass St. Andrews church on your right. On reaching some houses, you can at this point, turn left to make a stop at "The Carpenter's Arms" pub, (Friary Meux) which offers a varied selection of food. "The Mill House" on the corner is so called as it was part of the old windmill which once stood here.

To continue our walk, ignore the first path on your right, the Greensand Way, "GW", and continue on for a short distance to join the second footpath right which is marked, beside a car park opposite Stoneleigh Road. Stay on the footpath ignoring all crossing and joining paths. The path joins a wide track in front of a post marked by yellow arrows where you should carry straight on. At a fork in front of some trees bear left, following a yellow arrow and ignore a crossing path soon after. The path begins to descend through attractive woodland and shortly after passes a small pond on your right, to reach a junction of wide tracks beside a bench. Do not take any of the wide tracks but follow the narrow path almost directly ahead, i.e. the second path on your left, which runs parallel with a wide track on your right. This winds to the bottom of a shallow valley gradually bearing away from the wide track on your right. Sometime after, on entering pine trees, a footpath joins from the left.

On reaching a "T" junction, turn left and after approximately 15 metres just prior to a road, turn right on to a marked footpath. After a short distance take a signposted public footpath on your left (take care not to miss this), to continue slowly uphill. This winds through woodland and bracken to meet a drive way on to which you should turn left to reach a road. If you wish to visit "The Grasshopper" pub and the attractive hamlet of Moorhouse Bank on the way, turn right along the road which soon bends left in front of some picturesque cottages. Continue along the road which leads to the A25 and "The Grasshopper" pub. The pub which is a fairly recent creation, built in the 1950's, is made from artifacts rescued from derelict buildings in the local area, hence its unusual appearance. It is called grasshopper after the Grensham family who lived at "Titsey Manor" (on our walk). The grasshopper was the family crest.

To continue our route however, cross the road to a car park opposite and go straight ahead passing to the left of a small wooden sports pavilion. Stay on the main path as it descends and approximately half way down, turn right on to another prominent path. Follow this downhill ignoring all joining paths and at the bottom continue straight on with fields on your right to meet a small gate. The gate is on your right, be careful not to miss it, and is marked by a blue arrow. Pass through this to cross a field, passing through another gate to enter woodland and continue to reach a third gate on your right through which you should pass. Again take care not to miss this. Cross a small field to pass through a gate and continue straight ahead.

There are good views right at this point of the valley you have just followed. At the crest of the hill take time also to look behind for lovely views of Limpsfield Chart. At the other side of the field pass through a small metal gate on to a wide track between houses to reach the main road, the A25. Cross the road and follow the tarmac drive ahead, marked public bridleway and signposted to "Broomlands Farm". Follow the drive downhill crossing a road for lorries, to pass through the farm yard of "Broomlands Farm".

Just after the farmhouse ignore a wide turning left and continue straight on for approximately half a mile to cross the motorway, the M25. Immediately after crossing, turn left over a stile which can be easily missed, on to a marked public footpath. The path goes down steps and runs parallel to the motorway to lead into a field. Go straight ahead keeping to the perimeter of the field, to go over a stile into another field again keeping to the left hand perimeter.

Almost half way across the field turn right to go diagonally left away from the motorway. This path is signposted. There are particularly good views to the right of the North Downs and Titsey church. The church looks particularly beautiful and it is hard to believe that it caused uproar when it was built. One well documented description of the time includes, "mean looking ediface of brick and stone" and "without beauty or comfort".

Head to the right of a small brick building owned by East Surrey Water. Cross over a stile and continue on to a road which you should cross. Turn left along the road and after approximately 50 metres turn right over a stile at a footpath sign. Cross a stream via a wooden footbridge and go over another stile to cross a field ahead. Cross the stile at the other side and after a short distance a second stile to cross another field and pass through a gate.

Cross the next field going diagonally left heading for a stone house and pass through a small gate on to a concrete drive where you should turn right. You are now heading for "Titsey House".

The walk now follows 'The Titsey Trail", a walk through the grounds of "Titsey House". This path runs through private property and is kept open to the public by the generosity of the Titsey Foundation Trust who maintain the path. You will see a few collection boxes along the way to assist in the upkeep of maintaining the path, please be as generous as possible. Please note that if you intend to take a large group through the grounds the Foundation Trust do request that you notify them first. Dogs are also not permitted without prior notice.

i **Titsey House (OS. 406552 Map 187).** *There has been a large building on this site since Roman times when it was a villa, though the house you can see today dates from 1775. The parkland through which our route passes is privately owned by the Titsey Foundation, a charitable trust. The trust manages the park and maintains the paths through it. The park was originally the seat of the Grensham family, Sir Thomas Grensham being famed for the building of the Royal Exchange. It was later taken over by the Leverson-Gower family and it was one of the latter family members who discovered the remains of the original Roman villa. The church, the tower of which rises behind the house, was relocated to its present position during Victorian times. An ancient yew close to the house marks its original site. The house and parkland are a particularly pleasant part of the walk, the higher reaches are run as a nature reserve and in summer the route can be a carpet of wild flowers. The walk through the park affords constantly changing views of the house and lake, the best view points offering a bench for the weary walker. Incidentally, the name "Titsey" is derived from "Tit", a Saxon fairy.*

Just before "Titsey House" the drive bends round to the left and continues in front of an old walled garden and through a small gate beside a cattle grid. After the cattle grid turn right and immediately left past the stables to pass an old granary house on the left and cottages on your right. Follow the path as it winds uphill after the cottages, to bear left at the top and follow the brow of the hill in a westerly direction. This is a prominent path with excellent views in places of the Weald and "Titsey House" itself.

Continue on the path until you reach a crossing track signposted as Pitchfont Lane. Here there are more signs indicating "Short" and "Long" route, take the long route, i.e. going over the crossing track to continue straight ahead. As a point of interest, The North Downs Way goes up Pitchfont Lane to reach the highest point on its route, Botley Hill (267m).

The path continues along the top of the hill which was obviously badly hit during the great storm of 1987. After three quarters of a mile, the path bends left to go downhill, there are ropes to assist your descent.

The path leaves the woodland via a stile. After crossing the stile turn right to go over a second stile ahead which is marked by a white acorn, indicating you are back on the North Downs Way. After approximately 10 paces cross a third stile on to National Trust land, Oxted Downs. Take the path running along the bottom of the downs following a fence on your left. As the fence turns to the left follow this but then stay on the path ahead as the fence turns left again. As the path ends turn left to go steeply downhill to a stile, ignoring the first path and stile on your right.